WESTON-SUPER-MARE

PAST & PRESENT

SHARON POOLE

SUTTON PUBLISHING

Sutton Publishing Limited
Phoenix Mill · Thrupp · Stroud
Gloucestershire · GL5 2BU

First published 2006

Title-page photograph: Victoria Bowling
Club, May 1907. *(Mary Macfarlane)*

British Library Cataloguing in Publication Data
A catalogue record for this book is available from the
British Library.

ISBN 0-7509-4065-4

Typeset in 10.5/13.5 Photina.
Typesetting and origination by
Sutton Publishing Limited.
Printed and bound in England by
J.H. Haynes & Co. Ltd, Sparkford.

Aerial photograph of Locking Road, *c.* 1927. The building with the chimney in the centre is
the Electricity Generating Station and Tram Shed. Just to the right of it is Wesuma Art Pottery
with its chimney and kiln just visible. This was opened in December 1926 by Thomas Lemon.
Both these premises are bounded on the south by the GWR railway. North over the open fields
is the line of the Weston, Clevedon & Portishead Light Railway and then Milton Road. The
grove of trees is Wellsea Orchard. Centre top is Ashcombe Park, while to the right is Milton.
The houses of Ashdene Road are newly built and the Hazeldene Road Quarry is clearly seen
top left. Today all these fields have been developed with housing. *(Sally Huxham)*

CONTENTS

Keith Hollands paddling at Marine Lake, 1950s. *(Keith Hollands)*

INTRODUCTION

Change is natural and necessary for anything or anybody to grow. Every settlement has evolved over time. Some 300 million years ago this part of what became Somerset was a shallow tropical sea. Over the millennia, movements in the earth's crust caused the seabed to rise up into mountains. As the climate changed and this area turned into a desert, winds and sand wore the mountains down into softly rounded hills. Another few million years passed and an Ice Age descended on most of Britain. This was a period when rhinoceros, cave bears and herds of reindeer and mammoths roamed the ice sheets that covered this part of England. As the ice melted, forests grew and nomadic people hunted the deer and wild pigs, cattle and horses.

Gradually people began to settle in one place, farm the land and keep domestic animals. By the Bronze Age, approximately 2000 BC, metalworking had been developed. We know that people lived in what is now Weston-super-Mare at this time as the remains of their tools and funerary urns with cremated remains have been discovered around Ashcombe. By about 650 BC farmsteads were scattered along the southern slopes of the hillside and a large hillfort with stone ramparts had been built on the top of Worlebury. The Romans came and went, the Anglo-Saxons fought off Viking raiders, and by medieval times Weston had acquired its name, become a village and established a church. Miners invaded the village when the valuable zinc ore calamine was discovered on Worle Hill in 1566, but otherwise life went on much as usual for most residents until the late eighteenth century, when the English invented the seaside holiday and Weston was set to become a fashionable resort.

The changes up to this point took millions of years. However, from the early Victorian period onwards the pace stepped up and became relentless, growing faster and faster – until today, when nothing seems to stand still for a moment. It seems to be that fact above all others that defines the time we live in. And while in the past the developments were, in the main, seen to be for the better and were usually driven forward by local people themselves, changes now often feel as if they are forced upon us and are not always welcomed or seen to be an improvement. The vast housing estates that encircle Weston are one example, encouraged by government targets rather than for the benefit of the town and despite an almost overwhelmed transport and health infrastructure. However, one should also realise that 'Nimbyism' (the Not-In-My-Back-Yard syndrome) is not confined to the present time. One has only to read back copies of the local newspaper to see that people's attitudes remain essentially the same and that resistance to change seems to be universal. The case of the railway is a good example. Given the chance to have Brunel's new Bristol & Exeter Railway laid through the growing town, complete with railway station to bring in lots of business, the reaction of Westonians was a resounding 'No!' Have dirty, smelly steam engines pollute their bright shiny resort? Absolutely not. For over forty years Weston was a terminus at the end of a branch line, its effects still felt today as many intercity trains bypass Weston on the main line, rather than divert on to the loop line to Weston station. With the probable expansion of Worle Parkway into a transport hub it is even possible that Weston station will close altogether in the not too distant future.

However, Weston is still basically a lovely town that many locals take for granted. Letters in the newspapers constantly complain about the decaying Tropicana, Knightstone and Birnbeck Pier, the number of drug and alcohol rehabilitation centres, and the general state of decline in the town, but the more people complain and tell others that Weston is a mess, the prophecy becomes self-fulfilling – the tourist numbers decline further and there is a natural reluctance to invest time and money to build upmarket venues and housing. Certainly the loss of family hotels, guest houses and facilities has taken its toll, both economically and visually. Many would also argue that the rash of new traffic schemes, one-way streets and pedestrianised areas has also been detrimental, resulting in gridlock in the summer and more cars and lorries on fewer streets. But in return a huge amount has been done recently to brighten and improve Weston. Indeed, it was illuminating that while taking the 'now' pictures for this book, and after years of seeming neglect, everyone in Weston decided to undertake improvement schemes the moment this author set out with camera in hand. Scaffolding and skips were everywhere! It was noticeable, while trying to get clear photographs of buildings, the amount of street clutter about – direction signs, prohibition signs, lampposts, bins, CCTV cameras. . . . Now if only someone could come up with a coherent, 'joined-up' policy on street furniture it would make a huge difference to the visual landscape.

No one wants to live in the past, or indeed in a Victorian theme park, and there is no need to copy Victorian architecture. Modern designs can be fabulous and thought-provoking, while still offering a harmonious streetscape. By all means conserve the best of what we have, but we need to build for the twenty-first century and beyond. The Victorian terraces for artisans and tradesmen have given way to copies of Victorian terraces. Where are the eco houses with turf roofs and solar walls that you see on the continent and which blend so well with the landscape?

The pictures in this book illustrate what Weston was like, how it has changed over time, and what it looks like today. Although aware of the changes taking place on the streets on a daily basis, it was fascinating when the images were placed together to see just how much has altered, and in some cases how much is the same. Of course it isn't just buildings and streets that have undergone change – society and attitudes have evolved. Compare the clothes of sportsmen and women of seventy years ago with those of today and one wonders how they had the freedom to move, let alone play. The same is true of beach wear – covered from head to toe in 1900, to barely a wisp of a bikini today, although warnings of skin cancer may encourage people to cover up again.

As for the photographs, it was a constant delight to find how many amazing and previously unpublished pictures are still out there, and I am indebted to those who allowed me to borrow their precious family albums and photographs. At one stage, with six photo albums to work on, I felt I was almost living in the past and would come up for breath and see my surroundings as a surprise. Such is the power of old images to transport one to a different time. I hope you enjoy browsing these photographs as much as I have enjoyed searching for them.

Sharon Poole, 2006

1

Beside the Seaside

View of the Grand Pier, 1904. This picture of the pier under construction was photographed from the first-floor terrace around the pavilion. The view landwards shows Weston seafront from the Sandringham Hotel on the left, to the tower of Emmanuel Church in Oxford Street on the right. Total construction time for the pier was just seven months. Work began in November 1903 and the pier opened on 11 June 1904. *(Mary Macfarlane)*

The Grand Pier, from Regent Street, 1904. This view shows the pier shortly after its opening on 11 June, with construction debris on the left of the pier entrance. The pier was lit by electricity and a searchlight was mounted on the dome of the pavilion; it must have been wonderful sight when it first lit up. Over 20,000 people passed through the turnstiles on the opening day. On the right is Huntley's Beach Hotel. This picture was taken from an upper room in Lichfield House, which once stood on the corner of Beach Road and Regent Street. It was demolished in 1905 and the Bungalow Hotel built on the site. That in turn was demolished in 1925 to build the Grand Central Hotel. *(Mary Macfarlane)*

Entrance to the Grand Pier, May 2005. After 101 years the pier shows major changes in its appearance while the Beach Hotel looks much the same. A new pavilion was opened on the pier in 1933, after the original one burnt down in Weston's biggest ever peacetime fire. The pretty Edwardian entrance to the pier was replaced with this modern version in 1969. At the time of writing planning permission has been granted to replace the entrance buildings with a design more sympathetic to the pier. Cars have replaced the horses and wagonettes but it is still a busy junction. *(Sharon Poole)*

Children paddling on the sands, *c.* 1904. Behind the paddlers is the new Grand Pier and pavilion. The boats are flatners, used as fishing boats throughout the winter and scrubbed up for use as pleasure boats during the summer months. Their flat bottoms mean they stay upright when the tide goes out, and the shallow draught enables the boats to sail close to the nets to collect the fish on an ebbing tide. *(Sharon Poole)*

Donkeys on the sands, 2002. Beach donkeys are as popular as ever, having been giving tourists rides since the late eighteenth century. The animals were originally used by fishermen to haul the catches up the beach, but the early visitors began to hire them to ride out to local sights and nearby villages and so the concept of the beach donkey was born. The Magor family hold the concessions today, but the Trapnell family are probably the best known. *(Sharon Poole)*

On the Grand Pier, late 1920s. This picture has to have been taken between 1927, when the central shelter with seating was built, and 1930, when the Edwardian pavilion was destroyed by fire. The pavilion housed a beautiful 2,000-seat theatre. Productions included opera, musical comedy, music hall, Shakespeare, ballet and boxing. Among the famous stars that trod its boards were Anna Pavlova, George Robey, Vesta Tilley, Sir Ralph Richardson, Mrs Patrick Campbell, Dame Clara Butt, Jack Hulbert and Cicely Courtneidge. Outside the pavilion at first-floor level there was a wrap-around terrace on which visitors could stroll, admire the views or simply listen to the band in the bandstand in front of the pavilion. *(Mrs G. Ellis)*

On the Grand Pier, May 2005. This view shows the new pavilion, opened in 1933. After the old theatre burnt down there was much debate as to what to replace it with and where. Some people favoured a site closer to the landward end while others felt this would look unbalanced. In any event, times had moved on and so, instead of a theatre, the pavilion became an amusement hall, the largest on any pier in Britain. *(Sharon Poole)*

On the Grand Pier, 1950s. In the foreground, two of the girls from the fish and chip stall are taking a break. *(Mrs Phyllis Jones)*

Below: On the Grand Pier, 2005. Fifty years separates these two photographs. The original cast-iron railings have gone, to be replaced by rust-proof aluminium. Some of the original railings can still be seen, however, in North Somerset Museum in Burlington Street, Weston. They are very ornate with the embossed letters GPC, for Grand Pier Company, in the centre of each one. In the background, blocks of flats have replaced some of the larger mansions, notably Glentworth Hall and Villa Rosa. *(Sharon Poole)*

The Grand Pier, *c.* 1908. This photograph shows the 500yd extension built in 1907 to allow passenger steamers to berth. This made it the second longest pier in the country after Southend. Unfortunately the currents proved too strong and it was used just three times by steamers. The extension was dismantled in 1916, although a short section remains just beyond the pavilion. *(Mary Macfarlane)*

Opposite, above: The Grand Pier pavilion under construction, May 1904. The pavilion was not ready to be opened with the rest of the pier in June, taking another month to complete. Local resident Madge Frankpitt remembered, 'The Grand Pier was a special attraction. Every season they used to have a resident brass band. I remember my mother telling me there was a man called Herr Kandt who had a band before the First World War, but in my time [1920–39] they used to have military bands. The pavilion was a beautiful theatre and all the touring companies used to come with musical comedies. For sixpence you could go upstairs into the balcony and lean over and watch the shows – they called them Sixpenny Leanovers.' *(Mary Macfarlane)*

Opposite, below: Grand Pier and sands, May 2005. It is still a magnificent pier by any standards and is probably as well used today as in the past. At high tide it achieves perfectly that sensation of being out at sea on a ship but with no risk of feeling sick. On the sands a group of beach donkeys have just been unloaded from their transport vehicle and the beach stalls are setting up for the day. *(Sharon Poole)*

Birnbeck Pier with a White Funnel Fleet steamer at the northern jetty, *c.* 1905. Both the original jetties were badly damaged in a great storm that hit the town in 1903. The northern jetty was originally of wood, but was rebuilt in steel, 50ft longer and 5ft wider than the previous one. It opened in 1905. The southern jetty took longer to rebuild, and you can see it is still in a wrecked condition in this photograph. It reopened in 1909 but was dismantled permanently in 1923 so that a large concrete platform could be built on the island to increase the land area. Among the cluster of buildings, the clock tower is to the right, a bandstand is just left of the tower, and on the left is the undulating track of the switchback railway. *(Mary Macfarlane)*

Birnbeck Pier, February 2005. Today the pier is derelict and in grave danger of falling down. It has been through a succession of new owners with big ideas on how to restore and revive the Victorian structure, but nothing has yet come to fruition. The pier is unique in that it links an island to the mainland, and was designed by the doyen of pier designers, Eugenius Birch. The lifeboat, on the slipway to the left of the pier, is the only part of the pier maintained today and access to it is by a narrow strip of new planks laid by the RNLI. A local entrepreneur, James Scott, recently attempted to purchase the pier and develop it with a huge glass building on the island, linked to the land by a curved 'harbour wall' structure running along the northern side of the pier. This deal fell through, however, and we can only wait and see what will happen now. *(Sharon Poole)*

Phyllis Coombs and Phyllis North on Birnbeck
Pier, mid-1930s. Dressed in their best clothes,
these two are enjoying a day out on the pier.
Behind them is the pavilion, with the steamer
jetty off to the right. Birnbeck Pier suffered some
loss of business when the Grand Pier opened,
but could still offer steamer trips and a wealth of
funfair rides. However, when the new pavilion
on the Grand Pier was opened in 1933,
amusements were abandoned on Birnbeck and it
never again achieved the huge numbers of
visitors that it did in its heyday – almost
15,000 on August bank holiday Monday, 1892.
(Mrs Phyllis Jones)

Below: Birnbeck Pier, May 1998. This picture
shows the sad state of dereliction on the island.
It is even worse today. Note the lovely cast-iron
dolphin-shaped seat brackets. The new planks
laid by the RNLI to the lifeboat house stand out
very clearly on the left. (Sharon Poole)

Anchor Head and Birnbeck Pier, 1905. This interesting photograph shows the southern steamer jetty on Birnbeck Pier being rebuilt after it had been wrecked in the great gale of 1903. Progress was slow and it did not reopen for another four years. On the pier itself the switchback railway can clearly be seen. The buildings on the right are part of the Royal Pier Hotel. *(Denis Salisbury)*

Birnbeck Pier from Anchor Head, 2003. The southern jetty in the picture above was dismantled in 1923. The Royal Pier Hotel has grown considerably. It was built in 1854 as a hotel but spent its early years as Anchor Head School under the direction of Dr Godfrey. Traces of a rock-cut swimming pool for the use of the pupils are visible in the rocks below. By 1870 it was in use as a hotel, as it has remained ever since. Anchor Head is a popular sheltered cove for sunbathers. It used to be the ladies' bathing place as it was discreet and private. *(Sharon Poole)*

Prince Consort Gardens and Birkett Road, *c.* 1903. A view taken from the approach road to Birnbeck Pier, this part of Weston was originally known as Flagstaff Hill. It was laid out as public gardens in the mid-1860s by the Smyth Pigott family, who owned the land. As the family's fortunes waned towards the end of the nineteenth century, Cecil Smyth Pigott offered the gardens to the town. These terraces were then constructed to provide walks and seating areas – and to discourage noisy games that might devalue neighbouring properties! The excavated stone was used in the building of the seafront promenade. The timber and glass shelter was built in 1900 and bears an elaborate date stone in the centre gable. *(Denis Salisbury)*

Prince Consort Gardens and Kewstoke Road, 2005. This picture illustrates quite a few changes. The foreground railings have gone, probably for salvage during the Second World War. The shrubs have grown, and there is a new block of flats to the left of Rockwood. The shelter remains unaltered though, allowing uninterrupted views across Birnbeck Pier to Wales. *(Sharon Poole)*

Claremont Crescent from Anchor Head, *c.* 1905. This crescent was built in 1865 on the site of Claremont Lodge. Claremont Lodge was a five-bedroomed mansion with its own bathing house, overlooking the sea. It was built for Christopher Kingdon in January 1817. The 1822 guide for the town describes it as 'a beautifully situated lodging house'. The Bishop of Bath and Wells regularly rented the house. Gradually, however, the Claremont area was developed. The house was demolished in 1864 to make way for this crescent of five-storey villas. The architect was Hans Price and it took builder John Hawker two years to complete. *(Denis Salisbury)*

Claremont Crescent from Anchor Head, May 2005. The box-like additions to the roofline and ground floor do the architecture few favours and it is sad that the majority of the fine metal verandas have disappeared, although the salt air probably caused them to rust away. It is still an imposing crescent with unrivalled views. *(Sharon Poole)*

Print of Glentworth Bay and Birnbeck Road, *c.* 1855. The little castle-like building on the rocks was the bathing house that belonged to Claremont Lodge, the three-gabled house to the left of the Royal Pier Hotel. This print shows just how grand the early seafront mansions were, with their landscaped front gardens and sea views. On the hilltop the stone walls of the Iron Age hillfort of Worlebury can be seen. The woods were only some thirty years old at this time and had not grown to mask this important archaeological site. It was about this date that the site was first fully excavated. The finds, including human skeletons, charred grain and animal bones, may be seen in North Somerset Museum. This picture also clearly shows the natural beach. The promenade was not built until the 1880s and the Marine Lake some forty years later. Until then this was the centuries-old rocky shoreline known to local fishermen. *(Sharon Poole)*

Glentworth Bay, 2003. The biggest change here from the view above is the building of the promenade in 1886. This huge project was begun in 1883, but not extended as far as Birnbeck until three years later. In 1927 the Marine Lake was constructed, creating an area where it was always possible to paddle and bathe, even when the tide was out. The large villas lining Birnbeck Road are now all hotels or nursing homes. The tree growth on the top of Worlebury totally hides the hillfort from view. *(Sharon Poole)*

Claremont from Madeira Cove, *c.* 1903. In the centre of the picture are Claremont Wine Vaults, built in 1850, with Claremont Crescent rising behind them. On the road, the tram cables can be seen. Trams ran in Weston from 1902 to 1937, when the motorbus took over. The Marine Lake causeway was not built until 1927 so this part of the beach was still tidal at this time. *(Denis Salisbury)*

Rozel bandstand, 1950s. This area has undergone many changes over the years. In 1920 a small semicircular bandstand was built here, known as the Dutch Oven because of its shape. This sheltered the orchestra but the audience and conductor were left out in the open air – not so good if it rained! In 1935 the first Rozel bandstand was built, with some covered seating at the back. This was made possible by extending the promenade out over the beach, with a colonnade running underneath. In 1937 the bandstand was completely rebuilt, as in this picture, with a windscreen for the audience and raised seating at the back. The stage was in the square building in the centre of this photograph. *(Revd Peter Gregory)*

Birnbeck Road from Glentworth Bay, *c.* 1901. The villas pictured are, from the left, Grosvenor Villas, Rozel Villas, Elizabethan Villas (with the two gables), Corfield House, Sutherland House and Beaufort Villas. These mansions were large even for the time they were built, and most were soon used as boarding houses and hotels. The natural shingle beach can also be seen. Today these villas are hotels and nursing or residential homes for the elderly. *(Denis Salisbury)*

Madeira Cove, 2005. In the centre of the picture is the remaining part of the old Rozel bandstand. On 13 December 1981 a severe gale wrecked much of the promenade, including the colonnade at Marine Lake. The damage was so bad it had to be demolished, and with it the Rozel bandstand. This is the only remaining part today and operates as a café. Above and to the right is Rozel House, the new 48-apartment block that replaced the Rozel Hotel and Marlborough Holiday Flats in 2004. The Rozel Hotel closed in November 2001 after being run for some eighty years by the Chapman family. The name Rozel came from Rozel Bay in Jersey, where Albert Bodman, founder of the hotel and great-grandfather of the last owner, Tony Chapman, stayed for his honeymoon. *(Sharon Poole)*

Manilla Crescent and Glentworth Hall, *c.* 1903. Manilla Crescent was built in 1851. Glentworth Hall was built two years later for the Cox family. It later became Hazelhurst School before being converted into a hotel in 1926; it was demolished in 1973 and a block of flats built. A few years previously, planning permission had been granted to replace the building with Weston's first motel with flats combined but this scheme never went any further. Behind Manilla Crescent the tower of Holy Trinity Church is just visible. *(Denis Salisbury)*

Manilla Crescent and Glentworth Court, May 2005. The different paint colours and the various alterations to the roofline over the years mean that this crescent is now unrecognisable as such. In the background Holy Trinity Church is now the Elim Pentecostal Church. On the right Madeira Court is the name of the flats behind Glentworth Court. They are retirement flats for the over-fifties. *(Sharon Poole)*

Manilla Crescent, 1870s. Another view of Manilla Crescent shows how elegant these villas once were. The lane to the left led to a Parish Room, recently demolished and currently being developed with town houses and more flats. The signs on the left of the end building read 'Manilla Crescent No. 8' and 'Entrance at the side'. *(Sharon Poole)*

Manilla Crescent, May 2005. Once again the changes to these buildings, while looking good in isolation, have destroyed the harmony of the crescent. Most of the front gardens have been tarmacked to provide parking, and attic conversions have straightened the once-attractive roofline on all but four of the fourteen properties. *(Sharon Poole)*

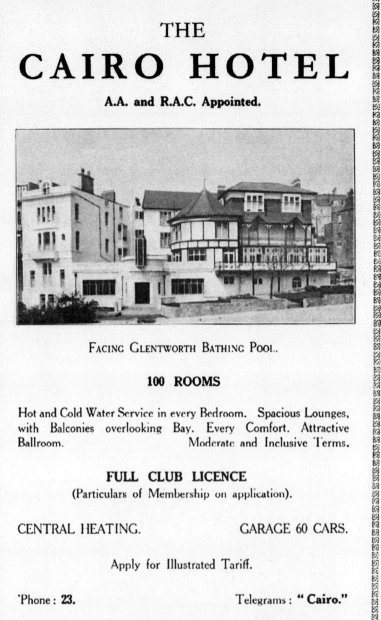

THE
CAIRO HOTEL

A.A. and R.A.C. Appointed.

FACING GLENTWORTH BATHING POOL.

100 ROOMS

Hot and Cold Water Service in every Bedroom. Spacious Lounges, with Balconies overlooking Bay. Every Comfort. Attractive Ballroom.   Moderate and Inclusive Terms.

FULL CLUB LICENCE
(Particulars of Membership on application).

CENTRAL HEATING.   GARAGE 60 CARS.

Apply for Illustrated Tariff.

'Phone : **23.**   Telegrams : **" Cairo."**

Advert for the Cairo Hotel, 1936. The Cairo Hotel began life as Devonshire Cottage, a small seaside villa built in 1821. When it was sold to Thomas Roblyn, a naval surgeon who retired to Weston, he renamed it Cairo Lodge in memory of the Battle of the Nile, in which he had fought. The building became a hotel in the 1920s and boasted scenes of pyramids and camels etched on the main glass doors. During the Second World War it was requisitioned as billets for the Brigade of Guards and in the run-up to D-Day in 1943–4 the US Marine Corps stayed there. Currently it is the Bayside Hotel. *(Sharon Poole)*

Princes' Buildings, Knightstone Road, *c*. 1904. This terrace was built in about 1842 and is one of three terraces fronting Knightstone Road, the others being Albert Buildings and Victoria Buildings. (*Denis Salisbury*)

Princes' Buildings, May 2005. A view remarkably unchanged aside from the loss of the first-floor balcony that once ran along the whole terrace. Cars have replaced horse-drawn carriages, of course, but nonetheless this is a scene our Victorian visitors would recognise today. (*Sharon Poole*)

Albert Buildings, Knightstone Road, *c.* 1900. This is the middle of the three terraces on Knightstone Road, built in 1843. The cast-iron street furniture is striking and the broad sweep of the empty promenade would indicate this picture was taken in the winter. In the road there is a horse-drawn carriage with two occupants, and in front a man pushing a hand barrow. Just to the fore of the barrow, one of the properties has an amazing arched gateway in topiary. At this date the properties are private dwellings or boarding houses. *(Denis Salisbury)*

Albert Buildings, May 2005. In contrast to Princes' Buildings, this terrace has changed greatly over the years. The properties are all now hotels and bars. An extra storey has been added to every house and the ground floors have been extended out to the front to create additional bar space and a terrace at first-floor level. *(Sharon Poole)*

Park Place from the Promenade, *c.* 1900. Park Place was one of Weston's most exclusive addresses when it was built in the early 1840s. Together with Greenfield Place and Royal Crescent it formed an elegant square with private gardens in front. These gardens were planted with specimen trees and shrubs and paths wound down to the seafront. *(Denis Salisbury)*

Park Place, May 2005. Today most of the properties in Park Place are hotels or nursing homes. Just one, the house on the left of this photograph, still looks as it did in the picture above. The private gardens that once fronted all these buildings have given way to a putting green and a council car park, although a few of the original specimen trees remain. *(Sharon Poole)*

Rough seas at Glentworth Bay, photographed by Ethel Hopwood, *c.* 1908. Before the Marine Lake was created in 1927, this was a popular part of the seafront to watch the waves crashing against the sea wall. Beyond Knightstone causeway there is a forest of masts from the boats in the harbour, while in the background is the Grand Pier pavilion and further in the distance, Uphill Old Church. *(Denis Salisbury)*

Knightstone and the Grand Pier from Marine Lake, May 2005. The seas no longer batter the promenade here, since the Marine Lake was built in 1927. Knightstone Theatre is derelict, as are all the buildings on the island, having been empty since 1992. In 2005 a scheme was finally approved to convert the listed buildings – the theatre, pool and Dr Fox's bathhouse – into apartments with some commercial use such as shops and bars. More flats will be built on the open areas of the island although public access will be maintained around the perimeter. *(Sharon Poole)*

The Drinking Fountain, Knightstone Road, *c.* 1900. Behind the fountain is the thatched Whitecross Dairy. This was built in 1791 as a holiday cottage for the Revd W. Leeves of Wrington. In the centre is the back of Royal Crescent, while on the right are Beachfield Villas, built in 1841 by Thomas Harrill on the site of Sheppard's farmhouse. At the time, they were reckoned to be much too grand for Weston and the rector told Mr Harrill that he would never find anyone with the means to live in them! One of those who did have the means in 1842 was Thomas Smith, one of the first town commissioners and a great public servant to Weston. In the right foreground is a drinking trough for the many horses that pulled wagonettes, carriages and carts up and down the seafront. *(Denis Salisbury)*

The Old Thatched Cottage Restaurant, May 2005. This is the second-oldest building in Weston after Glebe House, and the only one to retain a thatched roof. In the Weston-super-Mare Improvement & Market Act of 1842, all properties built after that date had to have a tiled roof as thatch could be a fire hazard. Also it was impossible to fit gutters to thatched roofs and so pedestrians were liable to get very wet walking past the older cottages. Beachfield Villas have both been extended and are now part of the Lauriston Hotel. The public drinking fountain and horse trough are now long gone. *(Sharon Poole)*

Royal Terrace from the Promenade, *c.* 1890. The couple in the carriage look well-to-do, with their own vehicle and driver. The gentleman is wearing a top hat and the lady is sheltering under an umbrella, as is the lady pedestrian behind them. *(Denis Salisbury)*

Royal Terrace, 2005. The building is pretty much the same as it was a hundred years ago, although it has had a coat of white paint over the stonework. The shrubs surrounding what was once the sunken tennis court for the Royal Hotel have gone. The Cabot Bars on the left, now a popular nightspot, were converted from an elegant Regency-style villa known as Esplanade Cottage and a later Victorian house. *(Sharon Poole)*

Royal Terrace and the Royal Hotel from the Grand Pier, 1904. This view, taken from the terrace of the Grand Pier pavilion, shows the open green spaces of Grove Park to the left and Rogers' Field to the right. The latter was the closest Weston got to a village green, and, until the 1850s, even had a duck pond and cows grazing on it. It belonged to the Royal Hotel which still holds covenants over the land, restricting the height of any developments and so protecting their views. *(Mary Macfarlane)*

Royal Terrace and Winter Gardens from the Grand Pier, May 2005. The Winter Gardens opened on 14 July 1927, providing a superb ballroom and entertainment venue. On the left is Weston College, the town's tallest building. It opened in 1970 and has invited controversy ever since partly because of its height, and also its uncompromisingly modern style. *(Sharon Poole)*

Rogers' Field and Victoria Square from the promenade, *c.* 1910. In the centre of this picture is the huddle of buildings that were the Royal Arcade, while the shrubs shelter the seaward end of Rogers' Field. The sloping ramp was built to enable bathing machines to be wheeled down to the beach. Samuel Harvey, who owned the rights to operate bathing machines from 1872, was loud in his protests when discussions took place in 1881 about the proposed new sea wall. His objections subsided when he was paid £200 in compensation and assured that the sea wall would be furnished with ramps so that the bathing machines could easily be drawn on and off the beach. The ramps remain and have been widened for the horseboxes that daily bring the beach donkeys on to the sands. *(Denis Salisbury)*

The York and Sandringham Hotels, Beach Road, *c.* 1903. On the right is Victoria Square with a glimpse of the first Daimler motor wagonette in the town. This offered 'pleasant motor rides' out into the countryside and surrounding villages. These vehicles gradually began to replace the old horse-drawn wagonettes seen centre and left. *(Michael J. Tozer)*

The York Convalescent Home and Sandringham Hotel, 2005. Both properties have had major alterations. The Sandringham in particular has lost two sets of elaborate bay windows and has had extensions built on to two sides. At fifty-four bedrooms, all en suite and with satellite television, this is one of Weston's largest hotels. There are also sixteen associated holiday flats. The York is a convalescent home run by the Royal Antediluvian Order of Buffaloes, Grand Lodge of England, for the use of lodge members and their families in need of rest and recuperation. *(Sharon Poole)*

Fella's kiosk, Beach Road, late 1980s. This stands in front of the mini-golf course in Victoria Square. Behind that is St Margaret's Terrace and the Salisbury Hotel, standing empty prior to demolition for the new Sovereign Centre shopping mall. (Sharon Poole)

Fella's fish and chip and ice cream kiosk, 16 September 2005. The kiosk and mini golf course are unaltered, but now the Sovereign Centre shopping mall provides the background. The tower was originally designed to house a scenic lift, but this was abandoned when costs had to be reduced. (Sharon Poole)

Beach Lawns looking south, *c.* 1916. Originally the whole of the Beach Lawns area was just windswept sand dunes. It was the influx of visitors brought by the railway from 1841 that persuaded the Town Commissioners this area should be improved. However, the ideas met a lot of opposition and nothing further was done at that time. In 1883, the new Seafront Scheme was started. This was for the construction of the 3-mile sea wall and promenade, and also included the landscaping of the Beach Lawns with grass and shrubs. Later, in the 1920s, the rockery was built down the western side to provide a windbreak. The first three houses on the left were demolished when the Grand Central Hotel was built in 1925. The frontage of the hotel was brought forward to street level, overshadowing the three properties on the corner of Richmond Street (see top picture on p. 38). The Boy and Serpent cast-iron fountain was made by the Coalbrookdale Factory in Shropshire. It was donated to the town by Thomas Macfarlane in February 1913. *(Revd Peter Gregory)*

Beach Lawns looking south, June 2005. The elaborate formal gardens with their corner gas lamps have been replaced by an expanse of grass. This is a popular spot in the summer for sitting and eating fish and chips. In the distance the Grand Atlantic Hotel is dwarfed by the towering bulk of Carlton Mansions. The fountain is a welcome survivor and in the background is the clock that used to be on the front of the Beach Road bus station (see p. 40). *(Sharon Poole)*

Above: Beach stalls, *c.* 1902. At this period there were some thirty stalls on the sands selling all manner of things, from seafood and ice cream to soft drinks and buckets and spades. In the past foreshore rights belonged to the lord of the manor whose agents generally allowed traders and entertainers to work unchecked. Eventually, however, there was so much happening on the sands – donkeys, fairground rides, sideshows, concert parties, stalls, even wild-beast shows – that some control was required. In the 1880s the town commissioners purchased the rights to the beach and brought in licensing. Trade was not allowed on Sundays and all stalls had to be removed every Saturday night to the respective owners' premises and returned on a Monday morning. *Below*: Beach stalls, 2005. Nowadays, beach stalls continue to sell seaside essentials while swing boats offer rides for young children and there are trampolines and go-carts. Trading is also now permitted on Sundays and bank holidays. *(Above: Denis Salisbury; below: Sharon Poole)*

The sands boating pond, 1920s. This was a gift to the town by Mr Leaver, who ran Leaver's ironmongery shop in the High Street. There is another similar pond at the southern end of the beach. *(Revd Peter Gregory)*

Boating pond, August 2005. There is so little difference between these two views they would be hard to date were it not for the clothing. However, while in the 1920s, the pond was used solely to sail model boats, here children are paddling and playing in the water. The pond now urgently needs repairs, and while the local authority recently considered demolition, it was decided to retain the pond for the present. *(Sharon Poole)*

Corner of Beach Road and Richmond Street, 1938. These properties were demolished soon after this picture was taken, with the intention of extending the Grand Central Hotel, which is on the left. The following year, however, the Second World War broke out and nothing further was done. The site took a direct hit from incendiaries and it remained a derelict site for the next fifty or so years. *(Mary Macfarlane)*

'Seven' Café Bar and Terrace, May 2005. This venture is pictured shortly after its opening. It is good to see the site finally developed. The end wall on the right belongs to what was originally the Atlantic Cable Office, now a nightclub. Several undersea communication cables came ashore at Weston and this office relayed the messages on to their destinations. During both world wars it was so important that the road was closed and permanently guarded, accessible only to those with a pass. *(Sharon Poole)*

The Oxford and Cambridge Hotels, Beach Road, Weston, *c. 1920*. These two hotels were on the corner of Oxford Street and Beach Road. They are typical of the early Victorian seaside villas that lined the seafront as far as the Grand Atlantic Hotel. Posters propped against the wall advertise cruises on the Red Funnel line steamers, sailing from Birnbeck Pier, while the property round the corner in Oxford Street is plastered with enamel signs advertising all manner of things from cider to Bovril. On the road you can see the tram tracks running up Oxford Street to Locking Road and the tram depot. *(Michael J. Tozer)*

Winston's Fish Bar, Beach Road, 15 September 2005. Until very recently this was Browning's rock shop. The Browning family held the beach tea-stall concessions and also made sweets and rock at a factory in Stanley Road. Raddy's, the bar next door, is named after Paulo Radmilovic, one of Britain's greatest swimming and water-polo stars. By the age of 45 he had swum in six consecutive Olympic Games, an achievement never surpassed. He represented Britain for the first time at the Athens unofficial Olympics in 1906. Two years later he was one of the gold-medal-winning 800m relay team at the London Olympics as well as winning a gold medal in the water-polo team. He won more water-polo gold medals in 1912 and 1920, making him the holder of the largest number of gold medals in Britain. When he retired from swimming he became a hotelier and restaurateur in Weston but still played water polo locally at Knightstone Baths. He died in Weston in 1968 at the age of 82. *(Sharon Poole)*

Beach Road, *c.* 1910. The large house to the left was on the corner of Carlton Street. Next to it is the tiny Camden Cottage; this was one of Weston's earliest holiday cottages. It survived into the 1980s before it was demolished, together with its neighbours. The house to the left of the Grand Atlantic Hotel is Belvedere. This was built in 1811 for Isaac Jacobs, owner of one of the Bristol glassworks, and was the first property built on what later became Beach Road. On the right is the Grand Atlantic Hotel. This was built in 1854 as a school. It was converted to a hotel in 1889 and is still in use as such today. *(Sharon Poole)*

Beach Road bus station, 1950s. This was built in 1928 on the site of Belvedere. In its turn the bus station was demolished in January 1988 following deregulation of the buses and amid much controversy. There is now no proper bus station for the town, just a couple of shelters in Locking Road car park and a 'bus focus' in High Street South. Carlton Mansions, Weston's largest block of apartments, now occupies the site from the Grand Atlantic Hotel to the corner of Carlton Street. *(Sharon Poole)*

2

Retail Therapy

T. Macfarlane & Sons' County Restaurant and Off Licence, Beach Road, 1904. This property, together with Lichfield House on the left, was demolished in 1905 and the Bungalow Hotel built on the site. Twenty years later that was in turn replaced by the Grand Central Hotel, which remains to this day, although no longer operating as a hotel. *(Mary Macfarlane)*

Widgery's chemist shop, 2 Fairlawn Buildings, West Street. This is one of the oldest chemist shops in Weston-super-Mare. It was opened in 1861 by George Gibbons, famous for his essence of seaweed, supposedly a 'safe and effectual cure' for anything from chilblains to tumours, lumbago to swelling of the glands! Gibbons ran the shop for twenty-six years, selling it to William Webb in 1887. Webb, then aged 32, moved in over the shop with his wife, son, two servants and a chemist's assistant. Chemists worked very long hours, including up to 8 p.m. on Sundays, and competition for business was fierce. By 1891 there were twelve chemists in Weston. Aside from medicines and potions, Webb also sold perfumes, toiletries, mineral waters, infant food and all manner of personal aids, including nasal baths. He also hired out water beds for invalids, used to prevent pressure sores. *(Sharon Poole)*

In 1897 George Stephen Ball took
over the shop. Ball already had a
chemist shop in Albert Terrace in
Weston but must have found trade
hard, since he sold this shop to
Ernest Widgery just four years later.
Two generations of the Widgery
family traded there for over
seventy-five years, before Ernest's
son, John, retired in 1971.
R.S. Medley then took over before
Shaw's bought the shop in 1988.
Many of the original shop fittings,
removed when the building was
modernised in the 1960s, can be
seen in North Somerset Museum.
(Sharon Poole)

Quinny's antique shop, West Street, *c.* 1961. This was one of the first antique shops in Weston. It was opened in 1963 by Laurie and Eileen Crews. Previously it was used as a fish and chip shop. In the 1970s, Weston was filled with antique shops, with two in West Street alone. *(Laurie and Eileen Crews)*

Snips hairdressers, 2004. After about twenty years the Crewses retired and the shop was sold. It is now a hairdresser's business. *(Sharon Poole)*

William Meakin with his daughter Gwen outside their premises in Baker Street, 1935. Meakin's was well known for second-hand furniture until October 1987, when the business closed. The buildings were demolished in 2004 and the site has been redeveloped with a block of flats. *(Mrs G. Ellis)*

Stephens coal yard, Baker Street, *c.* 1903. The posters on the wall advertise 'Best Speciality Coals'. The premises had frequent changes of ownership and a variety of uses over the years. In 1912, the owner was G. Davis, Furniture and Odds & Ends Stores. By 1918, Brooke & Prudencio were the occupiers. They were a mineral-water manufacturer, but whether it was used as a store or factory is not clear. In 1927, Wild & White were operating a removal and carriers business there, but two years later it was Reakes Garage. Reakes moved further along Baker Street and by 1931 Weston Trading Ltd were using the buildings for their corn chandlery. Then in 1932 it was taken over by William Meakin senior in order to expand his cycle repairs and carriers business next door. The Meakin family remained in ownership until 1987. (*Mrs G. Ellis*)

Gwen and William Meakin's shops, Baker Street, 1935. William Meakin senior took over this cycle-repairs business in 1925. The adjacent sweet shop was run originally by his sister Frances and then later by his daughter Gwen. (*Mrs G. Ellis*)

Bill Meakin's shop, Baker Street, 1960s. During the Second World War, William Meakin senior was awarded a contract to empty houses requisitioned for the war effort. Following the war he started a house-removal business, later expanding in second-hand furniture and 'junk'. You never knew what you might find exploring Meakin's yard – from three-piece suites to fine antiques. One regular visitor was Arthur Negus, the antique dealer of television fame in *Going for a Song. (Mrs G. Ellis)*

New flats, Baker Street, June 2005. Meakin's business closed on his retirement in October 1987. The following year the site was sold with planning consent to convert the existing old stables into housing. However, in 2004 the old buildings were demolished and this new block of seven flats built by Raglan Housing Association. These will be available to rent by local people. *(Sharon Poole)*

E. Bond & Co.'s Somerset Supply Stores, *c.* 1903. These provision merchants and corn stores were on the corner of Baker Street and Wooler Road. Baker Street was a thriving shopping centre serving the residential areas of Swiss, Jubilee, Wooler and Glebe Roads, and most items could be bought within a few yards. *(Andrew Palmer Collection)*

Baker Street launderette, June 2005. This launderette opened in 1963 and is still going strong today. The premises look little different from the picture above, although the roofline has been changed and the bay windows removed from the adjoining property. *(Sharon Poole)*

Upper Church Road, *c.* 1906. This small shopping area served the Shrubbery and adjoining roads. In 1909, it contained every trader one could need, including a chemist, fly proprietor, bootmaker, fishmonger and fruiterer, furniture dealer, two pubs (the Criterion and the Raglan Arms), grocer, baker, newsagent, dressmaker, greengrocer and refreshment rooms. The houses in the distance are the backs of those in Highbury Parade. *(Sharon Poole)*

Upper Church Road, May 2005. Today, many of the shops have been converted into residential use. The post office has moved three properties to the east and there is still an off-licence, two pubs and a general store, but no chemist, butcher or hairdresser any more. In 2000, while builders were converting the shop nearest on the right into living accommodation, they uncovered a beautiful old shop fascia board. In carved letters of black and gold it reads 'J. Arkell, Pharmaceutical Chemist'. J. Arkell was working at 51 Upper Church Road, or 4 Park Row as it was also called, in 1911. In the picture above, taken five years before Mr Arkell took occupancy, it is the building with the enormous gas lamp hanging over the door. *(Sharon Poole)*

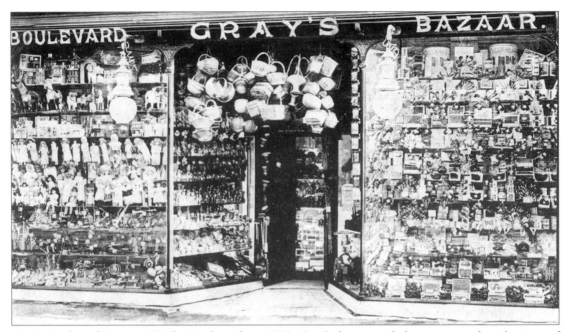

Gray's Boulevard Bazaar, 20 The Boulevard, *c.* 1906. Gray's fancy goods bazaar opened at the turn of the twentieth century. Before Mr Gray took over, the shop was a grocer's owned by Charles Harries. Mr Gray ran the bazaar until 1912, after which Mrs W. Gray was listed as the resident, joined a year later by a W. Govier. The shop window is fascinating and contains all manner of goods including dolls, baskets, toy ships, dolls' houses and model horses, to name but a few. *(Michael J. Tozer)*

Bengal Raj Restaurant, The Boulevard, August 2005. This was the site of Gray's Bazaar. As in most towns, Indian restaurants are very popular and there are now several in the town centre. This one specialises in Bangladeshi cuisine. *(Sharon Poole)*

Weston Decorators Supply Ltd, 27 August 1971. Weston Decorators was founded by Edwin Griffiths in 1936 in premises on Alexandra Parade. The business then moved to this shop on the corner of Orchard Street and The Boulevard. In the picture the property is for sale, prior to their move further up the street. This must have been photographed on a Sunday judging by the deserted streets. *(Sharon Poole)*

Interior of Weston Decorators' store, April 2003. In 1971 Weston Decorators moved from the corner of Orchard Street to these premises further along The Boulevard. The business finally closed in August 2003, on the retirement of the owners. Sadly it was not possible to sell the business as a going concern, with fierce competition from out-of-town superstores, so the shop was divided into two separate units. Domino's Pizza occupies the western half; at the time of writing the other part is still unoccupied. *(Sharon Poole)*

High Street looking north, 1905. On the right the shops included Lance & Lance and Walker & Ling, both well-known stores locally. Lance & Lance was Weston's largest department store until it suffered a direct hit during the Second World War and was never rebuilt. Walker & Ling are still going strong today, selling haberdashery, men's and ladies' fashions and drapery. The gas lamp illuminates the way to the post office. *(Michael J. Tozer)*

High Street looking north, June 2005. All the premises on the left of the Gardens Restaurant were rebuilt following bomb damage during the Second World War. The street is now fully pedestrianised, a fact the café has taken advantage of by putting tables and chairs outside. The tall pole with the CCTV camera testifies to social changes, unfortunately for the worse. *(Sharon Poole)*

High Street looking north, 1970s. On the left are John Collier and Keith Pople, both selling menswear, Salisbury's for luggage and handbags, and Marks & Spencer. On the right is Maynards' sweet shop, Liptons' grocers and Stead & Simpsons for shoes. Traffic was still allowed access, although it was one-way southbound, and it was possible to park outside some shops – a very distant dream today! (Sharon Poole)

Weston High Street looking north, June 2005. The buildings themselves have changed little. There are, however, more service industries such as travel agencies, opticians and mobile-phone shops rather than just retailers. The street is now closed to traffic and the central lamps with their attractive floral baskets certainly improve the streetscape. (Sharon Poole)

High Street decorated for Christmas, December 1962. This photograph was taken from the corner of Post Office Road looking south. The illuminated shop fronts look most inviting to window shoppers. *(Mary Macfarlane)*

High Street looking south, 2005. Ironically the pedestrianisation allows people more space to browse and window-shop at a time when window displays no longer seem to be fashionable. *(Sharon Poole)*

High Street North, early 1960s. These buildings were designed by local architect Hans Price and were completed in 1899. The structure was cleverly designed to incorporate the old 1827 Market Hall behind these properties with access through an elaborate archway to the left of Mr Gibson's shop. The Market Hall was converted into the Playhouse Theatre in 1946. (*Sharon Poole*)

High Street North, June 2005. The old Playhouse Theatre, converted from the Market Hall, burnt down on the night of Friday 21 August 1964 as a result of a carelessly discarded cigarette. It destroyed all but the front and side walls, both of which were unsafe and subsequently had to be demolished. Tenants lost everything from their homes above. It was described in the press as the worst fire in Weston since the Second World War. Afterwards, the Borough Council considered rebuilding the theatre somewhere else in the town but this idea was rejected. Instead, two properties in Worthy Lane were purchased so the site could be enlarged. The architects were Messrs W.S. Hattrell and Partners of Coventry. They created a versatile theatre with a 59ft stage and a cleverly designed orchestra pit which can be covered to form an apron stage or floored over at stalls level for additional seating. The auditorium seats 672. The decorative panels on the frontage were the work of sculptor William Mitchell, who also did work at Liverpool cathedral. The new theatre opened in 1969 with a production of *Let Sleeping Wives Lie* starring Brian Rix. (*Sharon Poole*)

Marks & Spencer's Penny Bazaar, 1908. This was the year Marks & Spencer first opened a shop in Weston, at 57 High Street. In the 1820s, this was the site of George Affleck's vegetable shop. A tiny shed-like structure with earth floor, it was nicknamed the Gentlemen's Club as every morning the gentlemen of the village would gather here to gossip and exchange news. *(Marks & Spencer Archives)*

Below: Marks & Spencer's shop, High Street, 15 May 1931. The shop hasn't really changed since it opened over twenty years previously. The only items on sale that are visible are a group of flags on the left and a folding paper Japanese fan hanging up. *(Marks & Spencer Archives)*

Marks & Spencer, 2005. The original shop, together with the neighbouring properties, including the Plough Hotel, were demolished in 1935 in order to build a new, modern and bigger Marks & Spencer store. The new shop was burnt out in 1942 when a nearby bakery was set alight by incendiary bombs and the fire spread. Marks & Spencer moved into temporary premises in Meadow Street where it remained until 1954 when the present shop opened in High Street on their original site. The 1954 shop front has worn well. The shop inside has been enlarged twice, once when the demolition of the Plough Hotel in Regent Street in 1972 provided space for a new food hall, and again when the Sovereign shopping mall opened in 1992. (Sharon Poole)

Building the Italian Gardens, 1923. Work began on developing Rogers' Field in 1923 with the first part – the Italian Gardens – completed a year later. As soon as workmen began to clear the site they encountered a problem. The ground was heavily waterlogged and had a virulent weed growth. One workman commented that it was worse than the mud of the Flanders battlefields in the First World War. Before the tennis courts could be laid, 6in of soil had to be removed, the area covered with concrete and the weeds treated with acid. This formal part of the scheme was separated from the Winter Gardens by a long terrace of Portland stone with statuary representing the four seasons. With this now in place it is impossible to reproduce this view today. In the High Street is Lance & Lance department store, Madame Windebank's millinery shop and Davies Brothers' stationers, all lost in 1942 to bombs. None of the buildings visible here in Waterloo Street survived the Second World War. *(Andrew Palmer Collection)*

Opposite, above: Building the extension to the GPO, Post Office Road, 1923. The main post office, between Cecil Walker's shop and this new extension, opened in 1899 on what was originally the site of Verandah House. The buildings in the right background are those of the Royal Arcade. These ran behind the High Street from beside Cecil Walker's shop through to Regent Street with a branch running at right angles to Salisbury Terrace. In the foreground is Rogers' Field, just before it was cleared to build the Winter Gardens and pavilion. *(Andrew Palmer)*

Opposite, below: The Sovereign Centre, 2001. In 1990, work began to demolish the post office, the remains of the Royal Arcade, Trevors' shop in the High Street and the multi-storey car park behind Marks & Spencer in order to build the new Sovereign Shopping Centre. This undercover shopping mall houses retail units, a café, and toilets with car parking above; it opened in 1992. While construction work took place, the formal rose gardens, tennis courts and putting green of the Winter Gardens were turned into a temporary car park. On completion they became the new Town Square, with seating, lawns and shrubs. *(Sharon Poole)*

Plough Hotel, Regent Street, *c.* 1958. This was actually an extension to the old Plough Hotel in High Street, where part of Marks & Spencer now stands. It was to the Plough Hotel that PC Robert Hill was taken in November 1847 after being stabbed by Tom Cann after a fracas at the corner of Regent Street and St James Street. Tom Cann was sentenced to seven years' transportation. PC Hill survived and even went back to police work, although he died in 1851 as a direct result of his wound. This is a superb example of an Edwardian pub with tiled façade and etched glass windows; inside was a huge mahogany bar. *(The late E.C. Amesbury)*

Marks & Spencer, Regent Street, May 2005. Marks & Spencer had been looking to expand their Weston shop for some time and the acquisition of the site of the Plough Hotel was a good opportunity. The old hotel was demolished in 1972. This photograph was taken after new traffic measures were introduced in the centre of town. Regent Street is now closed to all traffic other than taxis, buses and disabled drivers. *(Sharon Poole)*

Regent Street looking east, *c.* 1958. The Victoria Hotel was one of Weston's oldest inns, probably built in 1837, the year Victoria was crowned queen. It was originally a coaching inn with stables at the rear. In the distance is the Odeon Cinema, Weston's finest example of art deco architecture, built in 1935. *(The late E.C. Amesbury)*

Regent Street, June 2005. This whole area was earmarked for redevelopment in the 1960s, along with Union Street, now High Street South. In 1970, the multi-storey car park was built, with a Tesco store on the ground floor. The Victoria Hotel was demolished in 1981, when Tesco purchased the site for a planned extension. In the event Tesco moved further along the road to a new site once occupied by the Excursion station. The main post office then relocated from Post Office Road off the High Street to this new building. *(Sharon Poole)*

St James Street looking north, *c.* 1924. This was an important shopping street, especially for the residents of the Carlton Street area. Traders included a jeweller's, grocer's, sweet shop, butcher's, dairy, and fish and chip shop. On the right a sign reads 'Fudges, Noted Fried Fish and Fruit shop', an unusual mixture by today's standards. At the end of the road is the Plough Hotel in Regent Street (see also p. 60, top). *(Michael J. Tozer)*

St James Street looking north, June 2005. Today most of the properties are restaurants rather than shops. Traffic is one-way northbound from Oxford Street as far as Richmond Street. Despite many attempts, it was impossible to photograph the street as empty of traffic as it is in the above image. *(Sharon Poole)*

St James Street looking south, 1950s. The first three shops on the left all belong to the British Co-operative Society (BCS) and include a dairy and draper's shop. In the 1840s this street was Weston's red-light district, later becoming the main shopping area for the maze of cottages centred around Carlton Street. (*Sharon Poole*)

St James Street looking south, June 2005. The Co-op shops in the above picture were demolished in 1960. The Co-op store in the High Street was then extended back to St James Street. Today it is owned by T.J. Hughes. (*Sharon Poole*)

Cousins's butcher's shop, Clevedon Road, *c.* 1909. E.J. Cousins's first butcher's shop was in Regent Street. In about 1909, he moved to this shop at 80 Clevedon Road. When the First World War broke out, his wife continued to run the shop until 1921, when Mr Bond took over. The interior and exterior of the shop were covered in blue and white glazed tiles, with elaborate panels of pastoral scenes inside. Carved animal heads flanked the windows and doors. *(Michael J. Tozer)*

Clevedon Road, 2005. In the 1990s the shop and its living accommodation were converted into flats. The carved stone animal heads remain, however, testifying to its previous retail use. One of the wooden carved and gilded fascia boards was salvaged and can be seen in North Somerset Museum in Burlington Street, Weston-super-Mare. *(Sharon Poole)*

Eileen M. Beach's shop in Clifton Road, 1928 and 2005. Eileen Beach was born in 1911 in Amberey Road, Weston (see p. 117). She bought this shop in 1928 with a loan from her parents and ran it until she got married. Today, the shop is a launderette but is otherwise little changed. *(Above: Eileen Oxley; left: Sharon Poole)*

Meakin's greengrocer's and fruiterer's shop, Anstice Terrace, Alexandra Parade, 1903. Thomas Meakin is standing in the doorway with his daughter Lily. Thomas's brother Fred is in the foreground with his barrow. The following year, Fred emigrated to Canada. The pub next door is the Red Admiral. (*Mrs G. Ellis*)

Barber's shop, Alexandra Parade, June 2005. At some point the tiny shop has been enlarged with the addition of an upper storey. (*Sharon Poole*)

Stanton's electrical shop, Orchard Street, May 1988. This was an Aladdin's cave for anyone interested in radio equipment. Note the sign advertising Ultra radios, a brand that has long since vanished. *(Sharon Poole)*

The Curry Garden Indian restaurant, Orchard Street, June 2005. This restaurant took the opportunity of extending next door into Graham Stanton's shop when it closed. *(Sharon Poole)*

Palmer's butcher's shop, Meadow Street, 1984. Window displays of hanging meat are unusual today. This picture was taken in November, while walking home on carnival night. *(Sharon Poole)*

Palmers butcher's shop, Meadow Street, June 2005. The shop window has been taken out and the whole frontage is now open to customers. Palmer's is one of the few independent butchers left in Weston in the wake of the growth of supermarkets. *(Sharon Poole)*

Pfaffs, Meadow Street, *c.* 1958. This men's outfitter's was on the corner of Palmer Street and had been trading from these premises for nearly fifty years. Meadow Street was a vital and thriving shopping area with all you could need in the one street, from butchers and grocers to drapers and toy shops. *(Sharon Poole)*

The Playground, June 2005. The shop is still selling clothes, but now specialises in streetwear for young men and women. *(Sharon Poole)*

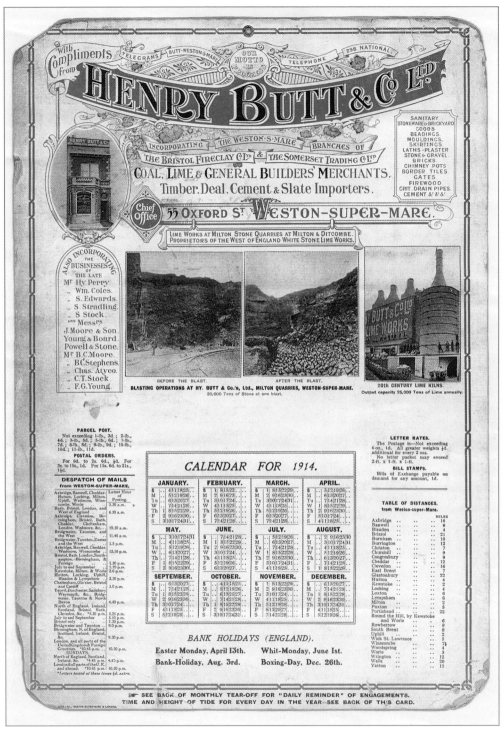

Henry Butt & Co. calendar, 1914. Henry Butt was a local entrepreneur who eventually became the town's first mayor, in 1937. He had fingers in many pies, including this lime works at Milton. He was a property developer, building several mansion blocks, particularly in the Shrubbery and Atlantic Road areas, and was also the principal fundraiser for a new hospital, which opened in The Boulevard in 1928. (*Michael J. Tozer*)

3

Fun & Frolics

Victoria Bowling Club, May 1907. This opened on 18 April 1900 and is the only club in the country to have provided three presidents of the English Bowling Association. Bowling is still a popular pastime in the town, with one indoor and two outdoor clubs. *(Mary Macfarlane)*

Crowds on the Beach Lawns for T4 on the Beach, 19 June 2005. This was a huge pop concert organised by Channel Four Television and broadcast live over an afternoon. Bands and singers included Daniel Bedingfield, Rachel Stevens, Athlete, Madness and Kaiser Chiefs among many others. More than 25,000 fans poured into the town. To entertain the crowds before and after the show, fairground rides were set up on the Beach Lawns. *(Sharon Poole)*

The Red Arrows over the Grand Pier pavilion, Great Western Air Day, 1989. The Great Western Air Days were very popular events, held annually for many years. Displays usually included the Red Devils parachute team, air-sea rescue demonstrations, aerobatics and the highlight of every weekend – the Red Arrows with their breathtaking display of sheer nerve. Memorable aircraft included the Vulcan bomber, which made every house in the town shake as it performed a low fly-past, and even on one occasion Concorde. *(Sharon Poole)*

Windsurfers, Marine Lake, 1987. Victorian visitors used the beach fairly sedately, strolling along the sands, riding donkeys, picnicking or possibly bathing. They might have taken a trip round the bay or listened to the band or concert parties. Today, these activities are still popular but much more use is made of the sea. At Weston, water sports include windsurfing, water skiing, jet skiing and sailing. For safety reasons this has meant different parts of the beach being allocated to different activities. This is not dissimilar from men's and ladies' bathing areas being kept well apart in Victorian times! *(Sharon Poole)*

Tom Davis, using a skim net on Weston beach in the 1950s. Skim nets were often used for fishing in the shallow waters of Weston and Bridgwater Bays and took a lot of strength and skill to operate. Tom's grandfather, George William Davis, nicknamed Jumbo, once caught a sturgeon off Weston. He set it up in a tent on the Beach Lawns and charged people to view it. As soon as he had raised £2, he shut up the tent and headed for the Coopers' Arms pub in Carlton Street! *(Carol White)*

Haile Selassie and his family at the
Severn Croft Hotel, Weston, July 1937.
Haile Selassie was born Tafari Makonnen
in Ethiopia in 1892. He married the
daughter of the Emperor of Ethiopia and
was named regent and heir to the throne.
In November 1930, he became emperor
and took the name Haile Selassie. He set
about modernising the constitution and
the country. However, despite treaties
with Italy, Mussolini invaded Ethiopia in
1935 and Selassie was driven into exile
until 1941. Much of this time, when not
seeking international support for his
country, was spent in Britain, and
Selassie and his family made a number of
visits to Weston. The Severn Croft Hotel
was on the corner of Beach Road and
Severn Road. More recently, it has been a
convalescent home but has been derelict
now for many years and it is due to be
demolished and replaced by a new British
Legion holiday and retirement home and
sheltered housing. *(Liz Batchelor)*

Museum Club carnival float, 1977. The summer carnivals were reinstated in 1958 after a break during the Second World War. They ceased again in the 1980s after the retirement of the main organisers and falling attendance. This float, entitled 25,000 Years BC and featuring a mammoth, was entered by the Woodspring Museum Club and is pictured outside the museum in Burlington Street before setting off. The Museum Club members were a group of about thirty children who met every Saturday morning for talks, activities and excursions relating to natural or human history. Every year they entered a float in the summer carnival, winning several cups for their efforts. Pictured front row, left to right, are Geoff Tozer, Graham Triggol, -?-, Edna Parkes, Sharon Poole, -?-, -?-, -?-, -?-, -?-, -?-. *(Sharon Poole)*

Opposite, above: Weston Carnival, *c.* 1903. Donkeys frequently featured in the carnival, either pulling decorated carts or being ridden as here. In the background the words 'Salvation Army' can just be seen written on the roof of the citadel in Carlton Street. *(Mary Macfarlane)*

Opposite, below: Weston Carnival float, 14 November 1912. This entry won first prize for the most original exhibit. It is pictured in Orchard Street outside No. 42, the shop of Mr Gabriel, undertaker and maker of window blinds. *(Mrs G. Ellis)*

The Olympians Concert Party in Grove Park, *c.* 1907. Cecil Smyth Pigott, last lord of the manor of Weston, sold 8 acres of his grounds to Weston Urban District Council in 1889 for the creation of a public park. The bandstand was erected in 1890 from prefabricated parts made at Hill Brothers' foundry in Alloa, Scotland, and the park opened to the public on 20 June 1891. Besides regular concerts, the bandstand became the focus for all kinds of celebrations from coronations and jubilees to Empire Day and, when Weston was granted borough status in 1937, the proclamation was read from this spot. *(Mary Macfarlane)*

Festival of Music and Dance from around the world, Grove Park, June 2005. For a period Grove Park was almost a no-go area with drunks and drug addicts. A concentrated campaign by the council, police and local residents has cleaned up the park and once again it has become a venue for open-air weekend events such as this festival. Every Sunday in summer bands play in the bandstand and special children's activities take place in the school holidays. *(Sharon Poole)*

Shelter in Grove Park, *c.* 1907. At this time the floral displays were very elaborate with 'rolls of carpet' and 'floral clocks'. The shelter here is lit, as is the fenced area, by gas jet lights encased in coloured glass shades. Even at this period, however, there were complaints about youths spitting and smoking in the shelter and that it was useless for invalids and visitors because noisy children were allowed to play there! *(Revd Peter Gregory)*

Shelter in Grove Park, June 2005. Today the shelter looks a bit bleak in comparison with the scene above. The seats have gone, as have the iron railings surrounding the lawn, and there are no longer any formal flowerbeds in this area of the park. The railings went for salvage in 1940. *(Sharon Poole)*

Arlotte's Weston Quavers, *c.* 1913. Concert parties entertained people with short sketches and songs and were performed on the beach on makeshift wood and canvas stages, or, if wet, under the pier. Others were performed on an open stage at Madeira Cove and in Grove Park. Later, pavilions were built so the show could only be seen by paying an entry fee. The audience paid 1*d* for a wooden seat or 2*d* for a deckchair. Every season there would be a different show at each venue. The Arlotte family were local. The group began in the 1890s with minstrel shows, moving on to concert parties as trends changed. They travelled all over the country with their troupe, training apprentices as required. *(Sharon Poole)*

Opposite: Trevor Schofield's dance classes, March 1953. Trevor Schofield first came to Weston during the Second World War as a pupil pilot in the RAF. He liked the town so much that on being demobbed in 1946 he got a job as a maths teacher at St John's School in Lower Church Road. His first dance classes were held in St Jude's Hall at Milton in 1947. He had such problems finding a venue to teach in the town itself that he was on the verge of emigrating to Canada when he was offered the ballroom of the Grand Atlantic Hotel. He continued teaching there until the hotel was sold to Trust House in 1957. He then moved to a permanent studio in North Street, in what was originally the function room of Browns Café. He and his wife Pat were pioneers in formation dancing and the Trevor Schofield Formation Team appeared for ten years on the BBC's *Come Dancing* shows on television. He retired in 1980 and the school closed. In thirty-three years more than 13,000 pupils attended classes in modern, Latin and old-time dancing. He died in April 1985 at the age of 69. *(Liz Batchelor)*

Soldiers of 'D' Battalion, 116th Anti-Aircraft Gun Battery, Beach Lawns, 1944. These US soldiers came over from America to Carrick Fergus in Ireland on the RMS *Queen Elizabeth*. After a few weeks' training, they then travelled to Weston, arriving on 7 December 1943. Battalion headquarters was the commandeered Severn Croft Hotel on Beach Road. That Christmas the men held a 'cash and candy' drive, pooling rations and raising enough money to buy fifty toys and a Santa Claus suit. On Christmas morning, Santa climbed into a Jeep and delivered the toys and sweets to local war orphans. In the New Year, they held training exercises and prepared equipment for the sea crossing to come. On 17 May, the full battalion left secretly at night. They headed for the mustering areas on the south coast, and landed on Utah beach in Normandy on 6 June 1944. Front centre is Corporal Francis Morris. The battalion commanders were Colonel Paul Morris and Colonel James Shearhouse. Note some local children getting in on the picture in the background! *(Liz Batchelor)*

The Coachmen's Dance Band, Royal Army Service Corps, April 1941. This photograph was taken when the band played on 25 April 1941 at the Kings Hall in Locking Road. From 1940 the Winter Gardens was closed for 'war work' and dances were transferred to the Kings Hall with George Locke and his orchestra the resident dance band. Pictured left to right are R. Gaskell, G. Biffen, L. Devine, J. McCleod, L. Can. *(Liz Batchelor)*

Stanmore House School pupils, 1898. It is believed this picture was taken in the Summer and Winter Gardens in The Boulevard. Stanmore House School was founded in 1848 in 7–9 Royal Crescent. It took both boarding and day pupils. In 1881, there were sixteen boarders out of the fifty or so pupils, coming from all over the West Country from Padstow to Swindon. The school colours were royal blue and red. In the 1930s, the school was run by the Misses Marion and Winifred Smith. At the outbreak of the Second World War, Weston was considered a safe place and the school continued to thrive. However, the bombing raids of 1941 and 1942 changed that and the boarding pupils soon left. After the war the school never regained its profitability and closed in 1948. *(Denis Salisbury)*

Ashbrooke House School, summer 1956. Situated in Ellenborough Park North, it was founded in 1953 by Kenneth and Margaret Thompson as a boys' preparatory school, with the aim of providing in a day school 'the amenities and training of a good boarding school'. In the early days, boys were admitted between the ages of 7 and 10 with fees of between 15 and 18 guineas per term. On leaving, the majority of pupils went on to public schools such as Charterhouse, Rugby and Winchester. Girls were first allowed entry in the 1960s. Today there are approximately eighty pupils taught by nine full-time staff and seven visiting teachers. Ashbrooke House School is one of only two surviving private schools in Weston today. *(Mrs Burrows)*

Weston Lifeboat *Colonel Stock* on its slipway on Birnbeck Pier, *c*. 1907. This is the longest slipway of any lifeboat station in Britain, because of the high rise and fall of the local tides. The lifeboat house, slipway and boat itself were funded by a legacy from the late Anna Stock of Weston. Until 1902 the lifeboat station was on the north side of the pier. It was decided to build the new boathouse on the southern side as it was easier to launch the boat at all states of the tide. This is still in use today. The boat was christened *Colonel Stock* after Anna's husband and was in use from 1903 to 1933. (*Sharon Poole*)

Weston Lifeboat Open Day, August 2005. The RNLI is run entirely on public donations. Since the lifeboat station is inaccessible to all but the crew, owing to the poor condition of Birnbeck Pier, an open day is held each year to raise funds and allow people to see the boats. Weston has two lifeboats; a 'D'-class inshore boat named *Faith* and an Atlantic 75 named *Coventry and Warwickshire*, as it was funded by donations from that part of the country. Both boats are called out regularly during the summer, most often for holidaymakers who get stuck in the mud trying to walk out to the water at low tide. (*Sharon Poole*)

4

Getting About

Uphill Junction, *c.* 1900. A 0–6–0T tank engine is heading up a train bound for Weston.
The driver is waving out of his cab at the photographer, Mr Macfarlane. The Bristol & Exeter
line, of which this is a part, was, like the Great Western Railway, built in Brunel's broad gauge
of 7ft ¼in. He believed it gave a more comfortable and stable ride, unlike the standard gauge of
4ft 8½in used elsewhere in the country. However, it caused major problems at places where the
two different gauges met. For a short period a third rail was laid to provide a dual gauge, but
the lines were fully converted to the standard gauge in 1896. (*Mary Macfarlane*)

Weston station, 1950s. This is the view that once greeted anyone standing on the railway bridge in Drove Road, near its junction with Locking Road. Weston was a busy railway station, with goods traffic and three passenger platforms. To the left, the track bends round into the main passenger station. A line of coal trucks is waiting on the siding behind the signal box. To the centre is the main goods station, while round to the right are the excursion platforms; these were built in 1914 to take the long trains full of day trippers, and prevent them blocking the main station. *(Sharon Poole)*

View from Drove Road railway bridge, August 2005. The changes between this view and the one above are quite dramatic. Gone is the maze of tracks and all that remain are a siding and the two lines into Weston station, hidden here behind Hildesheim road bridge. The signal box and coal trucks have been replaced by a car showroom – highlighting the change in transport culture from rail to road. Again to the right, a coach and car park has replaced the excursion station and goods yard. *(Sharon Poole)*

Milton Halt, 30 August 1990. Milton Halt was opened on 3 July 1933 as a commuters' stop, and is still in use. The platform itself looks much the same today, but the hedges on the far side of the line now mask part of the huge new Locking Castle housing estates, in particular The Barrows. The bridge over the line carries Locking Moor Road to Banwell. *(Ann Deakins)*

Worle Parkway railway station, 2 August 2005. Worle Parkway was opened on 24 September 1990, as part of a park-and-ride scheme serving the residents of North Worle. Today it is increasingly well used by those in the new housing estates in St Georges and around Summer Lane. There was a previous Great Western railway station in Worle in 1884, just off the junction of the main railway line and the loop line into Weston; it closed in 1922. Additionally, the Weston, Clevedon & Portishead Light Railway ran through Worle with a halt in Station Road close to the Worle Gas Works. *(Sharon Poole)*

Motorbus, late 1920s. This bus was new in 1920 and is painted in the smart dark-blue and white livery of the Bristol Tramways & Carriage Company, with the Bristol coat of arms on the side. The first regular motorbus service in Weston began in 1912, operated by the BT&CC. The gradual expansion of these operations signalled the end of the trams, limited as they were to a fixed route, while buses could travel anywhere. The last tram ran in Weston on 17 April 1937. The destination board on this bus reads Fore Street, via Southend Road and the Town Hall. Fore Street in Milton, was renamed Baytree Road in 1932. *(Michael J. Tozer)*

A motorbus dating from about 1908 outside the Town Hall, early 1920s. Note the 12mph limit just above the running board! The destination board on the side of the bus reads 'Woodland Rd, Clevedon Rd, Town Hall for GWR Station, Light Railway, Ashcombe Park'. The Weston, Clevedon & Portishead Light Railway ran from its terminus on the corner of Milton Road and Ashcombe Road via Milton and Worle to Clevedon and on to Portishead. It opened in 1897 and ran until 1940. The Town Hall is pictured before an extension was built in 1927. *(Michael J. Tozer)*

Tram on Beach Road, 19 July 1921. This is one of the 'toast-rack' trams with open sides. These were generally only used in summer; striped roller blinds could be dropped down from the roof to protect the passengers from sudden showers or hot sun. The conductor would stand on the running board along the sides to collect the fares. Weston also had a fleet of double-decker trams with open tops. Trams operated in Weston between 5 May 1902 and 17 April 1937, when motorbuses finally forced the closure of the tramway. *(Michael J. Tozer)*

Buses in High Street South, June 2005. This spot in High Street South is as close as Weston gets to a bus terminus and is closed to all other traffic. The main office for the local franchise holder, First Bus, is behind the photographer. *(Sharon Poole)*

Bristol Tramways & Carriage Company bus, May 1934. In 1930 the speed limit for buses was raised from 20mph to 30mph. The following year a licensing system for public service vehicles was brought in and drivers could be required to take a test at the discretion of the Traffic Commissioners. The test was not compulsory until 1934. It looks as though the driver has sneaked his young daughter on to the top deck of this bus for the photograph! *(Michael J. Tozer)*

Advertisement for motor charabanc tours, 1920s. Charabancs were the motorised equivalent of the old wagonettes. The hood could be folded back so everyone got a good view and lots of fresh air. Note the booking office in the Plough Garage. This was at the rear of the Plough Hotel in Regent Street (see p. 60). *(Michael J. Tozer)*

Motor Charabanc Tours from Weston-super-Mare.

A Fleet of the Famous Dennis 28 Seater
"Pride of the West"
Torpedo Charabancs For Hire.

Tours Daily during the Summer Season, to places of interest ——————— Cheddar, Wells, Glastonbury and Minehead ; also long tours to Bournemouth, Torquay, Weymouth, etc.

CENTRAL BOOKING OFFICE—
Plough Garage, Regent Street.

Special Terms for Parties.

PROPRIETOR—
A. E. ATYEO, Hatfield Road Garage, WESTON-Super-MARE.

Below: Beach Lawns looking north, *c.* 1930. Coaches are lined up ready to set off on day trips. All but one have had their canvas roofs folded back so passengers can enjoy the fresh air. Note the lady on the balcony of the Crown Photographic Studios, on the right (see also p. 38). *(Sharon Poole)*

Hovercraft on Weston beach, 1963. This was a short-lived experiment in running a regular hovercraft service between Penarth and Weston. The operator was P. & A. Campbell, who also ran the steamer services but felt that the days of the paddle-steamers were numbered. The tickets cost £1 per person and the journey took 12 minutes. The service was dropped after one season. (*Ann Deakins*)

MV *Balmoral* at Knightstone Island, 2003. Steamers have been taking passengers on excursions from Weston since the 1820s, embarking them originally from Knightstone Island and then, from 1867, Birnbeck Pier. By the turn of the twentieth century, sometimes 6 to 8 ships could be seen queuing to disembark passengers at the pier – up to 15,000 people a day! The last scheduled sailing took place on 19 October 1979 owing mainly to the poor state of the Welsh piers and the collapse of Clevedon Pier. However, on 27 May 1989, Clevedon Pier was reopened with a special cruise on the paddle steamer *Waverley*. Today, she and her sister ship *Balmoral* run summer season cruises every year, embarking passengers again from Knightstone as a result of the poor state of Birnbeck Pier. (*Sharon Poole*)

5

Weston Town

South Parade and the Winter Gardens from the post office, *c*. 1934. The circular part of the garden was planted with roses and gave off a lovely scent in summer. In the foreground is the sunken garden with statuary and shrubs. The half-timbered building was the pay booth for the tennis courts. Lloyds Bank is still in the same building on the corner of South Parade and the High Street. The three houses just to the left of it were demolished in 1964 to enlarge the bank, and the gardens and tennis courts were removed in 1990 for the extension to the Winter Gardens. The remainder of the area was used as a temporary car park during the construction of the Sovereign Centre and now forms the Town Square. *(Revd Peter Gregory)*

Dorville House, Madeira Road, *c.* 1916. Originally named Sutton House, it was built in the early 1850s. The first occupant was Samuel Baker, son of the founder of a local firm of solicitors and steward of the manor of Weston. By the start of the nineteenth century, it belonged to Miss Baker, presumably Samuel's daughter. In 1914, Miss Baker died and Thomas Macfarlane moved in with his family. Thomas died there in 1921. The next occupant was Leonard Guy, who was general manager of the Grand Pier. In 1933, the house was sold to Frederick Whiting. He and his wife Dede converted it into a hotel and renamed it Dorville House. *(Mary Macfarlane)*

The Dorville Hotel, 1960s. The original house, which can just be traced from the two bay windows in the centre, was considerably enlarged in 1952. Joe Whiting, son of Frederick, took over the business in 1962 and ran it until it closed in September 2002. The building was sold to the Bristol Family Housing Association and for a short time was used as a hostel for the homeless. In July 2004 planning permission was granted to demolish the building and replace it with twenty-two flats. *(Marina Coles)*

Rockwood, Birnbeck Road, August 1906. This house was built in the 1850s, on an elevated site with a commanding view across Birnbeck to Wales. In the 1881 census the owner was Joseph Hughes, a 36-year-old carpet manufacturer from Kidderminster. He lived there with his American wife Amelia, son Charles and two daughters, Edith and Clara, a cook and a housemaid. He must have spent some time in the USA himself since his first child, Edith, was born in New York City. In this picture several garden urns and some statuary can be seen. It is likely these were made in Weston at the Royal Pottery in Locking Road. Similar items are illustrated in surviving catalogues. *(Mary Macfarlane)*

Rockwood, Birnbeck Road, 2005. Today, like most of the larger houses in Weston, Rockwood has been divided into flats. The formal lawns have been terraced and tarmacked to provide car parking spaces. On the left a block of flats has been built in what was part of the garden. *(Sharon Poole)*

La Retraite Roman Catholic School for Girls, South Road, *c.* 1970. This building began life in about 1859 as two villas, Holywell and Woodlands. In 1881, Holywell was owned by Charles Girdlestone, a retired rector, or, as the census so charmingly put it, a 'Clergyman Without Care of Souls'. His sister Charlotte lived next door at Woodlands. Woodlands later became Forest Hill School and Holywell was opened as Coombe Ladies' College, run by Miss Astle. By 1910, the two houses were being run by Mr Ibbs as a boys' school. He retired that year and La Retraite Convent, which was operating a girls' school in Fortfield next door (see p. 97), was able to purchase Woodlands and Holywell. The large house on the right was Dunmarklyn, also a private school for many years, before being taken over by La Retraite for dormitory accommodation. *(Community of La Retraite)*

Rainham Court, South Road, June 2005. This was the site of La Retraite School, which closed in 1971 at a time when many private schools were struggling to attract sufficient pupils to survive. The 1970s was also a period when Weston lost many of its largest and oldest buildings – Etonhurst, Villa Rosa and Kingsholme to name just a few – and La Retraite was no exception. It was demolished in 1986 after several years of dereliction. *(Sharon Poole)*

La Retraite Convent, *c. 1910*. This house at 65 South Road was originally called Fortfield. From 1894 to 1900 it was the home of William James and his family. William James was the father of Ivy Millicent James, a renowned children's postcard artist. When they left this house, the La Retraite Convent took over the building to use as an elementary school for approximately thirty pupils. *(Community of La Retraite)*

Leawood Court, South Road, June 2005. The house has had a name change but is essentially unaltered on the outside, even retaining the fine cast-iron balcony railings. The flats on the extreme left have been converted from the La Retraite School chapel. *(Sharon Poole)*

Inwood, South Road, 1958. The large mansions along South Road were nearly all built between 1858 and 1867 on plots released from the manorial estate. By 1864, some of the homeowners were extending their gardens by buying up more land on the hillside and cutting across some of the Iron Age fortifications in the process. This house was listed in the 1861 census as 'nearly built'. Ten years later, it was in the occupation of William Holt, a captain in the militia, with his wife, four children and four live-in servants. However grand the houses were, the road was a different matter. By 1879, the surface had become so bad that the local authority invited tenders to sort out the drainage, kerbing and metalling of the roadway and charged the costs to the house owners. *(Revd Peter Gregory)*

Abbey Grange Nursing Home, June 2005. Like many of Weston's hotels, Inwood has now become a nursing home for the elderly. The castellated bay windows and porch have disappeared under a glazed conservatory structure, but the upper half of the building is largely unchanged. *(Sharon Poole)*

Above: Holland House, South Road, *c.* 1920. This house was built in about 1861. William Ash, a landowner and solicitor, lived here for many years with his wife, brother and four servants, including an Italian butler. From 1917 the house was used as a dormitory for St Peter's School, those sleeping here being known as the Holland House Butterflies. The pupils moved to the main school when it was extended in 1924 and Holland House was sold. *(Michael Freedman)*

Holland House, 2005. The house was sold by St Peter's School in 1924 and was extended and converted into flats about 1933. Since then the garden has been excavated down to fully expose the semi-basement and to provide parking. *(Sharon Poole)*

St Peter's School, *c.* 1908. St Peter's School was founded in 1882 by the Revd R.F. Duckworth as a preparatory boarding school for boys, although later on day pupils were taken as well. By 1906, pupil numbers were growing and so a new school was built on a site at the end of Shrubbery Avenue. It was constructed from a design by Ward & Cogswell of London, and built by Robert Wilkins & Sons of Bristol. Probably the best-known ex-pupils of St Peter's are Roald Dahl and John Cleese. Friends remember Roald, an avid smoker from a very young age, making cigarettes from the Virginia creeper climbing up the walls of the school. *(Michael Freedman)*

St Peter's Avenue, May 2005. St Peter's School closed in 1970, at a time when many private schools were struggling to survive. The building was demolished and the housing estates of St Peter's Avenue and St Matthew's Close built on the playing fields and school site. The tall building in South Road is Holland House, a dormitory for St Peter's school from 1917 to 1924 (see also p. 99). *(Sharon Poole)*

The cricket pitch at St Peter's School, *c.* 1908. The 5-acre playing field was advertised in the prospectus as one of the best and driest in the county. As well as this field for games such as cricket, football and rugby, there was also a gymnasium for PT and boxing, a tennis court and a swimming pool. *(Mary Macfarlane)*

St Matthew's Close from South Road, June 2005. When St Peter's School closed in 1970, it was not long before the school was demolished and the land sold for building. In many ways it is now greener and probably a lot more wildlife-friendly than it was as a playing field. *(Sharon Poole)*

Gardeners Lodge, Shrubbery Avenue, 1911. Originally called East Lodge, this pretty Gothic-style cottage was built in the early 1840s for the gardener of the Villa Rosa estate. The gate on the left led to glasshouses and what was probably the original kitchen garden for Villa Rosa. Behind the cottage is St Peter's School. Pictured left to right are Mr Daffern, his wife Emily, daughter Catherine, aged 2, and son Thomas. *(Mrs Elver)*

St Peter's Avenue and St Matthew's Close from Shrubbery Avenue, 29 August 2005. There is now no trace of any of the buildings in the 1911 photograph. This estate was built in the 1970s after the closure of St Peter's School. *(Sharon Poole)*

Villa Rosa Housewifery School, 1933. Villa Rosa was built in 1845 for the Misses Pank. They were so taken with Weston (they said Weston Bay reminded them of the Bay of Naples) that they sent over an Italian architect to design their new house. However, no sooner was it finished than Sophia Rooke purchased it. The mansion was the centrepiece of a private estate. Access was via Upper Church Road and South Road, guarded by lodges and toll gates. There was no access then, as there is now, from Highbury Road until 1871. Plots were sold off and large villas built. The housewifery school was formed in 1922 by Mrs Laws as an offshoot of Eastern House School in Landemann Circus. There were just six girls to start with; by 1933 there were twenty pupils who came from all over the country to take a one-year course in running a household. *(Michael J. Tozer)*

Villa Rosa, Shrubbery Road, June 2005. Planning permission to build flats on this site was first applied for in 1962. This was followed by several changes to the design scheme, including a group of three-storey blocks, a crescent-shaped block of forty flats, and even three tower blocks. The block to the left was finally built in 1972. The developers then went bankrupt so the second block was built a year or so later by another company, hence the difference in design. *(Sharon Poole)*

Overcombe, 24 Shrubbery Road, May 2005. This interesting property has been under threat of demolition since the 1970s. At the time of writing a planning application to replace it with a block of fourteen flats has just been refused, but its future is uncertain. Overcombe was built in about 1841 by John Perry, a local builder and sometime partner of Samuel Harvey, another local builder and developer. It was designed in the Victorian Gothic style and built, unusually for Weston, of brick rather than the local limestone. Even more interestingly the bricks are not of the orange-red local clay and may have been imported, possibly from Bridgwater. The interior is grand and boasts at least two white marble fire surrounds. In the census of 1861 and 1871, the resident was Rachel Bennie, a gentlewoman and widow born in the West Indies. In 1881, the owner was Frances Townsend, a 41-year-old widow from Ireland living off income from land. She lived there with her mother, also named Frances, her cousin Mildred and daughters Henrietta, Elizabeth and Joanna. The staff consisted of a governess, housemaid and cook. During her occupation the house was enlarged with a new east wing. Frances died in May 1891 and the house was sold to William Bennett. He also was a man of means. His children were born in Ceylon so he may have served with the East India Company or owned tea or rubber plantations. By the turn of the century, the house changed hands again and at the time of the Second World War had been converted into four flats which is how it remains today. Sadly the majority of the building has been allowed to become derelict and currently there is only one tenant in residence. *(Sharon Poole)*

Atlantic Road, *c.* 1890. These five-storey terraces were built in the 1860s as large family homes, maintained by live-in staff. Note the gates have all been offset from the main entrances to give an elegant curved sweep to the front path. The balconied building at the end of the terrace is Eastern Mansions. One of the apartments, No. 6, was the childhood home of John Cleese. In about 1955 the Cleese family moved out and Jeffrey Archer and his parents moved in. *(Sharon Poole)*

Atlantic Road, May 2005. Over a hundred years of growth of the trees and shrubs in this picture has all but hidden the buildings, but it is nice to see that these gardens have not all been lost to car parking. The terrace also remains easily recognisable, although the once-grand houses are too big for today's families and have been divided into flats. *(Sharon Poole)*

Shrubbery Garage, 1985. This was built as a mews and livery stable for the large houses in the Shrubbery Estate and South Road. Many of these properties had their own coach house but would keep their horse at livery. As horse traffic declined in favour of the motor car the business changed from horses to horsepower and became a motor garage. *(Sharon Poole)*

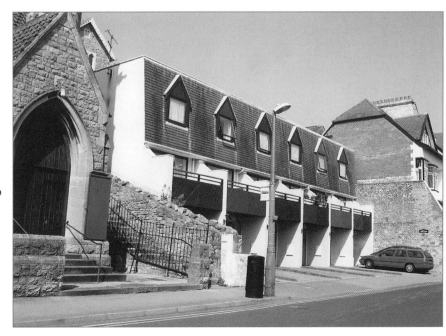

Shrubbery Mews, Upper Church Road, June 2005. Shrubbery Garage could no longer compete with the main dealers and closed in the mid-1980s. Many smaller garages also closed at this time as big new showrooms and dealerships opened on the outskirts of the town. These town houses were built in 1986. *(Sharon Poole)*

Moroccan-style house, Grove Park Road, 1901. These semi-detached villas, pictured under construction above, were designed by local architect and builder Walter Wooler. They were inspired by a visit he made to Andalusia in Spain. The ogee-shaped windows and ceramic tiles, imported from Spain, show a pronounced Moorish influence. Today, despite loft conversions, the houses are still an interesting architectural oddity in the town. *(Above: Mary Macfarlane; below: Sharon Poole)*

Grove House, Grove Park, *c.* 1910. Grove House was once the summer cottage of the Smyth Pigott family, lords of the manor of Weston. The house saw many famous visitors over its life as a manor house, including author Wilkie Collins. In 1889, the last lord of the manor, Cecil Smyth Pigott, moved back to his main home of Brockley Hall near Bristol, and advertised The Grove for sale as building land. The Town Commissioners persuaded Cecil to allow the town to acquire the land for the creation of a public park at an annual ground rent of £300. It opened on 20 June 1891. The house was used variously as a library and café before it was destroyed by bombs during the Second World War. The men in the picture are the team of gardeners required to maintain the park with its elaborate carpet bedding displays and rock gardens. *(Sharon Poole)*

Grove House, Grove Park, 26 June 2005. In both January 1941 and June 1942, Grove House was hit in major bombing raids. The remaining shell, with the exception of the coach house, was demolished in 1952 and this bungalow was built four years later. Today, it houses the mayor's parlour and offices of the town council. There are plans to restore Grove House to its original appearance and to use it as a register office among other functions. It remains to be seen whether this will attract sufficient funding or not. *(Sharon Poole)*

South Parade, *c.* 1869. These elegant residential properties were built in 1819. On the left is Myrtle Cottage, once home to Samuel Serle. Serle was an entrepreneur of astounding versatility. On a small watercolour portrait, painted in the 1850s, it lists his occupations as 'Parish Clerk, Sexton, Town Councillor, Beer and Cider seller, Brick & Tile maker, Public Library Keeper, Print Seller, Stationer and Toy Seller, Fisherman, Boatman, Hairdresser and Barber, Perfumier, Farmer, Grazier, Milkseller, Theatre Manager and Lender of Carriages and Chairs for Hire'. Myrtle Cottage was demolished in the 1870s and a bank built on the site. The Bath Hotel was also built in 1819 and was originally called the Masons Arms. In Brown's 1854 guide to the town he wrote, 'The Bath Hotel, situated in a line of pleasant houses in South Parade, is ably and genteelly conducted by Mrs Wookey. This establishment has an air of privacy, which renders it peculiarly inviting to families loving quiet and retirement.' It was here in 1865 that William Terriss, later to become a famous actor, stayed when he was mistakenly thought by locals to be the Prince of Wales. (*Sharon Poole*)

South Parade, June 2005. Today the properties have all been converted to commercial use. In about 1870 the Bath Hotel was renamed the Imperial, which it remains to this day. Competition between the Imperial Hotel and Royal Hotel was always fierce, as they are so close geographically, and the story goes that since the only person to outrank a king is an emperor, the name Imperial was chosen, to indicate its superiority over the Royal! (*Sharon Poole*)

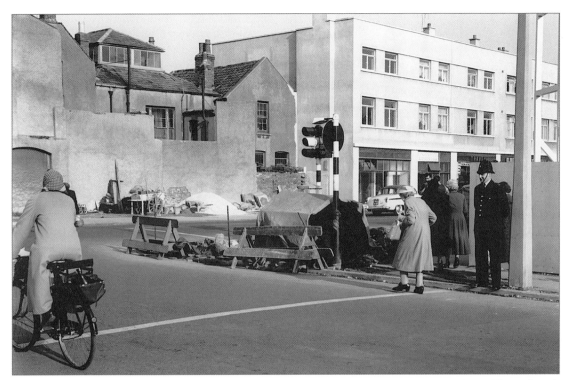

Corner of High Street and Waterloo Street, 1952. This shows the aftermath of Second World War bomb damage. On the right stood Lance & Lance's department store which suffered a direct hit on the night of 28 June 1942. Only the lift shaft remained standing. In Waterloo Street some rebuilding has already taken place. To the left is the exposed wall of the London Inn and the backs of properties in Worthy Place. (*The late E.C. Amesbury*)

Corner of High Street and Waterloo Street, February 2005. Trees planted in the Italian Gardens and in the High Street itself soften the hard landscaping of the paving and railings. At the time of this photograph, new paving was being laid and a new pedestrian crossing made over the road to High Street North, which had just been closed permanently to traffic. (*Sharon Poole*)

The National School, *c.* 1880. This stood on the corner of Knightstone Road and Lower Church Road. It was built in 1846 mainly at the expense of Bishop Law, a benefactor to Weston in many ways. In fact the official opening of the school was postponed owing to the illness and subsequent death of the bishop. There was accommodation for 160 boys and an equal number of girls, although by 1873 there were well over that number of regular pupils. Parents paid 2*d* a week or 1*d* if more than one child in a family attended. In 1897, the boys' department moved to the newly built Board School in Walliscote Road and for a time there were only girls here. On the extreme right can be glimpsed the end of Oriel Terrace and a walled plot. The School of Science and Art was not built until the 1890s. The National School, by then known as St John's, was demolished in 1966. *(Sharon Poole)*

Weston College, February 2005. The technical college was opened on 11 September 1970 by Viscount Amory as a tertiary vocational college. Long before the government's emphasis on lifelong learning, the then principal, R.S. Mason, said that 'Weston-super-Mare flourishes by the industry of its people. By increasing their knowledge and skill the College will enrich the town as a holiday resort and aid its growing industry.' In 1998, it underwent a major facelift. The long flights of steps at the main entrance were removed and the entrance relocated at the side. The building was also painted and given new windows, both of which soften its previous stark exterior. *(Sharon Poole)*

School of Science and Art, *c.* 1899. In Weston, evening classes for adults began in 1873 with science classes given in the National School at the bottom of Lower Church Road (see opposite page). In 1882, a Government School of Art was opened in the Church Institute in The Boulevard. This was well subscribed with over seventy students and it was decided to mark the Diamond Jubilee of Queen Victoria with a new purpose-built School of Science and Art. A site was chosen next to the National School and the project was funded by donations and grants. The new building was designed by local architect Hans Price and opened in 1893 with 110 students. An extended façade was added a few years later. Today, it is the art department for Weston College. *(Denis Salisbury)*

The Boulevard looking east, *c.* 1902. On the left is the corner with Longton Grove Road. In the distance the spire of Christ Church can just be seen, while coal merchant Mr F. Harvey's delivery cart is being driven towards the photographer. *(Denis Salisbury)*

The Boulevard, July 2005. One hundred years separates these two views but the road essentially is little different. There has been infilling with a block of flats below Christ Church and the gas lamp has given way to modern street lighting. The main difference is in the traffic, both type of vehicle and volume. There has been a lot of debate recently about the lovely cherry trees that line the street. Many are old and the council feels they would be better felled and replaced by saplings of a different species. However, the scene in spring, with the pink and white blossom, is stunning and would be greatly missed. *(Sharon Poole)*

Summer and Winter Gardens, The Boulevard, *c.* 1920. The idea of a Winter Garden for Weston-super-Mare dates back to at least 1881. In August that year, the Town Commissioners discussed the idea of a place for people to go to enjoy the autumn and winter sun as the weather grew colder, and where entertainment like fêtes, concerts, lectures and sports could be provided. And so the Summer and Winter Gardens opened on 16 August 1882. It underwent several changes of use, including concert hall, roller-skating rink, cinema and theatre. It was finally destroyed by bombing on 28 June 1942. *(Revd Peter Gregory)*

Tivoli House flats, June 2005. After the old Tivoli Theatre was destroyed in the blitz of summer 1942, the site lay derelict for nearly fifty years. Finally it was developed in 1984 with this block of flats, offices and a retail unit. *(Sharon Poole)*

Lauriston House from Royal Terrace, c. 1910. This was originally two houses. They were amalgamated and turned into a hotel in the 1930s. The Lauriston became the first Action for Blind People hotel in 1964 and was officially opened by Princess Alexandra. This was only the second specialised hotel for those with impaired sight in the country, the other being at Bournemouth. Special adaptations allow visually impaired people to enjoy a holiday in Weston either alone or with their relatives and partners. All thirty-eight bedrooms are en suite and have talking alarm clocks as well as the usual televisions, radios, cassette players and telephones. One facility that stands it apart from other hotels is that there is a special shower and grooming room for guide dogs, and dog beds, fleeces and bowls are available in each room. The exterior looks little different today, apart from the front garden being used for parking. In the right foreground are the glasshouses of Weston Nursery run by Mr Ellis. (Denis Salisbury)

The Beach family, Amberey Road, 1912. William Beach and his wife and daughter Eileen pose outside their house at 28 Amberey Road. Eileen was born in the house in 1911. When the houses were built in about 1905, the road was named Amberley Road, although this could have been a misprint in the street directories. By 1910 the name had been changed or corrected to Amberey Road. At that period it was a cul-de-sac with apple orchards at the end of the road. The houses look little different today, aside from some modernisation such as new windows, but the orchards have long since been built upon and the road is no longer a dead end. *(Above: Eileen Oxley; left: Sharon Poole)*

Everley Villa, 35 Clevedon Road, *c.* 1902. This is one of the many hundreds of small semi-detached villas or 'cottages' as they were called at the time, built to the south of the town for the 'respectable working classes'. The sign in the window reads 'Apartments'. Letting rooms in the season was an easy way for families to supplement their income. *(Revd Peter Gregory)*

No. 35 Clevedon Road, June 2005. The property is now Everley Villa Guest House. The building itself has lost a few of its architectural features over the years, including the decorative ridge tiles, gable finial and attractive parapet over the bay window. It has also lost its fine gateposts. Some of the changes could well be the result of bomb damage, as this area suffered several hits in 1941 and 1942. *(Sharon Poole)*

Maxdene, 35 Severn Road, 1908. This is a classic Victorian villa, built from the local limestone, with Bath-stone facings and decorative elements such as the carvings between the floors on the window bays. Such attention to detail even included the finials on the gate pillars. From about 1903 until 1927 the owner was T.E. Macfarlane, son of Thomas Macfarlane who lived in Sutton House (see p. 94). It was he who took this photograph, with his wife and children outside. *(Mary Macfarlane)*

No. 35 Severn Road, 2005. Today this villa is part of Lyndhurst Park Care Home for the elderly. Externally it is largely unchanged, apart from the plethora of television aerials on the roof. It has also been linked to its neighbouring villa with a side annexe, as well as being extended at the rear. *(Sharon Poole)*

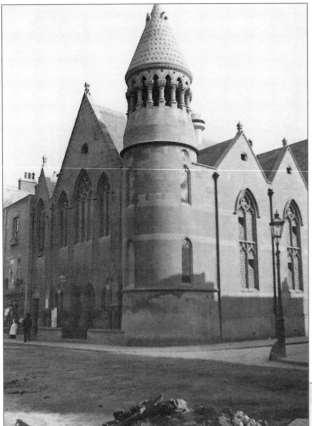

Above: Regent Street Wesleyan chapel, *c.* 1900. The foundation stone was laid in 1846 at a time when the town was rapidly expanding. The chapel underwent some rebuilding and the addition of a spire some twenty years later.

Right: The chapel finally closed at the end of the nineteenth century and was converted to commercial use, and is seen here in 2005. By 1903 it had become a bank. Most of Weston's disused churches and chapels have been adapted to a new use, including the Wadham Street chapel, now a theatre, and the Boulevard Methodist church, now an estate agent's. (*Above: Denis Salisbury; right: Sharon Poole*)

Beach Garage Café, *c.* 1937. This was on the first floor of the Beach Road bus station, with a view out over the seafront and beach. The bentwood chairs, china and vases of flowers evoke the pre-war era beautifully. This café was run by the Woodley family during the Second World War; they also owned cafés in the Royal Arcade and Regent Street. *(Liz Batchelor)*

Alfred Street looking north, *c.* 1904. On the corner of Burlington Street is Vowles Bakery. The road looks remarkably quiet and empty in comparison with this spot today. *(Michael J. Tozer)*

Alfred Street looking north, June 2005. Little has changed here aside from the fact that the busy junction is now controlled by traffic lights. *(Sharon Poole)*

Wooler Road, *c. 1918*. This street was named after Walter H. Wooler, a local architect and partner of Hans Price. The attractive terraces are a matching pair. The setting looks positively rural but then at this date there was very little built beyond Ashcombe Road so Wooler Road was almost on the outskirts of Weston. In fact, when Georgina Shorney married Harry Payne in about 1900, and he bought a new house in Baker Street for them to live in, she insisted they move as it was too far out in the country! *(Michael J. Tozer)*

Wooler Road looking north, June 2005. Today, this small back street is usually filled with parked cars, as this photograph shows. At the end of the road, in place of the trees in the above picture, there is the rear of the telephone exchange. This was opened in 1967 at a cost of £530,000. It saw the changeover from a completely manual service to one that was almost entirely automatic and required new telephone numbers for the whole town. Until this building opened, the manual telephone exchange was operated from an upper floor in the main post office, with a small relief exchange in The Boulevard. *(Sharon Poole)*

Magistrate Courts, Walliscote Road, 2005. This neoclassical building was opened in 1934, together with four police houses to the right of it in Walliscote Road. The latter were demolished when the new police headquarters was built in 1969. On the left can be glimpsed the tower of the Victoria Methodist Church. (*Sharon Poole*)

New Court and Probation Service Building, 2005. This new complex on the outskirts of the town at Worle has been designed to house five courts as well as the regional headquarters for the National Offenders Management Service and replaces the existing courts at Weston and Flax Bourton. The £15-million high-tech building is equipped with video conferencing facilities. It is due to open in May 2006. (*Sharon Poole*)

The Campus, Locking Castle, September 2005. This flagship scheme won an international design award in 2005. The striking building is a new concept in north Somerset and brings together several services under one roof. Heron's Moor Primary School caters for 420 children while Baytree Special School has room for 67 children with severe learning difficulties. There is also a library, community information and technology facilities and a police office. The two schools share some facilities such as the sports hall, hydrotherapy pool and dining area and this encourages the pupils to mix with each other. There is also a café area and community rooms which can be used by local clubs and societies. In the evenings and school holidays, the sports hall, dining hall and kitchen facilities are available for use by the community. Built at a cost of almost £11 million (£2 million over budget), it occupies an 11-acre site in Bransby Way. The building has been in use from September 2004 but was officially opened by HRH the Princess Royal on 10 October 2005. *(Sharon Poole)*

Defusing an unexploded bomb, Stradling Avenue, 1947. This was one of several high-explosive bombs that were dropped on Weston on the night of 28 June 1942. That night saw the second major blitz on Weston, destroying large parts of the town and killing many people. Among the damage and debris, unexploded bombs littered the streets, including one on the seafront and one which, instead of exploding, had burst its casing, scattering explosive content across a busy street. In part of the attack it appeared the enemy was targeting the transport system as bombs fell close to five of the six road bridges over the railway, although none hit their targets. This is one of those bombs. *(Mrs Phyllis Jones)*

6

Milton, Uphill, Worle

Worlebury post office, 1995. The proprietor, Sid Jones, is pictured in Worlebury's original post office, which he ran from 1963 to 1995. Sid was also an expert car mechanic and clock mender; in fact, as Ann Deakins remembered, 'What Sid didn't know about wasn't worth knowing!' Sid died in 2004. *(Ann Deakins)*

Worlebury post office and shop, 29 January 2000. This was situated on the corner of Milton Hill and Worlebury Hill Road. It had been a shop since the 1920s, when J.D. Payne ran it, but only became a post office in 1998 after the closure of the one in Monk's Hill. *(Ann Deakins)*

Milton Hill, May 2005. Both shop and post office closed in February 2004, leaving just a pillar box by the bus stop. In December 2004, the bay and shop front were removed and the building returned to purely residential use. *(Sharon Poole)*

Worlebury Lodge, *c.* 1920. This tiny gamekeeper's or woodsman's lodge was built in about 1823. The hill above Weston was naturally bare of trees, like Sand Point and Brean Down. It was John Hugh Smyth Pigott, lord of the manor, who decided to create a wooded area as a private game reserve. The public were allowed access to walk, ride and admire the views, but not to shoot or trap game. Anyone found poaching would suffer the consequences, and the practice was severely discouraged – at Milton Mr Bisdee was known to lay a mantrap in his grounds! *(Sharon Poole)*

Worlebury Lodge, 1987. When the manorial estates were sold off in 1914, the lodge became a private residence. It has also been at times a café, as in this photograph, and an antique shop. *(Sharon Poole)*

VE Day party in Furland Road, 8 May 1945. Street parties like this one took place all over Weston to mark the end of the Second World War in Europe. Rations had been hoarded and were pooled to create a 'victory tea'. Public houses were allowed to stay open until midnight and as night fell, the 'victory lights' went on as the blackout was ended and buildings could again be floodlit. There was dancing and music in the streets and parks until the small hours. *(Ann Coia)*

VJ Day party in Furland Road, 15 August 1945. Victory over Japan and the final end to the Second World War was celebrated on this day; despite the poor weather, this was too important an event to go unmarked, although there were not the same celebrations as there had been in May for VE Day. The large numbers of children in this picture probably include evacuees. Approximately 10,000 children and expectant mothers came to Weston and the immediate area on the outbreak of war and many stayed here after the armistice. *(Ann Coia)*

Furland Road, Milton, between 1939 and 1945. At this time, the road was surrounded on three sides by the market gardens for which Milton was famed. The newspaper placards help to date this image with headlines like 'War Debt confusion in Washington', 'Roosevelt War Sensation' and 'Air Liner disaster, 6 men missing'. *(Michael J. Tozer)*

Furland Road, Milton, 2005. The post office is now a tanning studio and the hairdresser's and newsagent's is now the Sunshine Store. At the end of the road the extent of the quarrying at Milton Hill can be seen in the changed profile of the hillside. Hundreds of tons of limestone have been quarried away here. The rock was blasted from the hillside, crushed and mixed with tar to produce tarmacadam. From 1926 onwards, concrete products such as fence posts, drainpipes and building blocks were made from the fine grit left by the crushers. Operations ceased in 1970 and the area has since been developed with housing, namely Ashbury Drive and its offshoots. *(Sharon Poole)*

HAWTHORN HILL
WORLE

The Garden Estate with magnificent Views

Facing south, with maximum sunshine, fully sheltered from all cold winds and in delightful surroundings, this Estate is reserved for a definitely limited number of houses, and will enjoy its own tennis courts and other amenities.

Plans for purchasers will be prepared, free of charge, to individual requirements if desired, and houses erected from £650.

Plots of one-eighth of an acre from £100. Other plots on the Uphill Park Estate. There are also available plots in the rural surroundings of Wolvershill, Banwell, Bleadon Hill.

BUILDING CONSTRUCTORS (Som.) Ltd.

1 THE CENTRE, WESTON-SUPER-MARE
TELEPHONE 1501

Advert for the new estate in Hawthorn Hill, Worle, 1935. This was developed by A.E. Lock as a garden estate. Mr Lock was already well known as the developer of Stanhope Road, The Centre and the Ellenborough Estate close to Weston railway station. Plots at Hawthorn Hill started at £100 for an eighth of an acre or it was possible to purchase a house, designed to one's specification, from £650. Only a limited number of houses were to be built, together with communal tennis courts for the use of estate residents only.
(Denis Salisbury)

Hill Road, Worle, *c.* 1902. In the centre is the parish church of St Martin, built in the twelfth century. In 1829, it was described as 'a small antique building, plainly but appropriately ornamented'. The church underwent considerable 'restoration' at the hands of the Victorians, but still has some interesting features, especially the fine, carved stone pulpit. At the top of the road on the left was Worle Elementary Board School, which opened in 1865. At the time of the photograph, there were two classes of twenty children each. As well as the basics of reading, writing and arithmetic, the boys learnt gardening on the allotments surrounding the school while the girls would have been taught sewing. Children left at the age of 12, most of them going straight into work either on the local farms or into service. *(Sharon Poole)*

Hill Road, Worle, 26 June 2005. Today, the view is recognisable only by the angle and slope of the road. Hillside School has expanded, with additional classrooms to the left. The open fields are now built upon and there is only the smallest glimpse of the chancel of the parish church. *(Sharon Poole)*

Coronation Road, Worle, *c.* 1905. This road was named in 1902, the year Edward VII was crowned king. The road surface is unmetalled and there are no pavements. The house at the end of the road is West Acre, then the residence of Dr St John Kemm. Note the bare hillside with a quarry to the left. *(Sharon Poole)*

Coronation Road, Worle, 26 June 2005. The road has seen little change, aside from coats of paint on the exterior render of several buildings. West Acre, which stood at the end of the road, has been demolished and Victoria Lodge flats built. Since the quarry ceased operations in 1970, shrubs and trees have softened the landscape. *(Sharon Poole)*

Lawrence Road, Worle, *c.* 1910. A tranquil rural scene of stone cottages and a fine elm tree. In the centre on the photograph is the Ebenezer Chapel, built in 1836. Worle's police station was also in Lawrence Road at about this period. A delivery boy poses with his bicycle on the left of the road. *(Michael J. Tozer)*

Lawrence Road, Worle, 26 June 2005. This view can only really be recognised by the Ebenezer Chapel, now Worle Community Centre. The cottage on the right in the above picture has been demolished and Lawrence Court flats built. The elm tree was probably the victim of Dutch elm disease, which felled so many trees in the area. *(Sharon Poole)*

The Square, Worle, *c.* 1907. Behind the photographer is the New Inn (now the Woodspring). This was a coaching inn, built in 1814. Here extra horses could be harnessed to coaches to make it up the steep Scaurs, seen in the picture. When the foundations for the inn were being dug, an ancient gilded bronze stirrup iron was found indicating the road has probably been in use for centuries. Note the unmetalled surface with puddles of water. The tiny corner shop is Worle Coffee Rooms, run by Mr Pearne. Up the Scaurs on the right, you can just glimpse some whitewashed cottages. These were almshouses for the poor of the village. *(Sharon Poole)*

The Square, Worle, 26 June 2005. This has to be the busiest traffic junction in Worle today. The almshouses and cottages on the left of the photograph above were demolished in order to widen the road, and a new block of shops and a bank were built in 1973. This was all part of the planned expansion of Worle with the new housing estates north of the village. *(Sharon Poole)*

Bristol Road, Worle, *c.* 1910. This picture shows Worle as it was – a rural village with unsurfaced roads and no pavements. Charles Bidwell recalled the village in about 1906: 'I well remember the white dusty roads. Candles and paraffin lamps were the only means of light in the cottages. All water was fetched from the village pump and we enjoyed the beautiful sight of horse-drawn carriages of holidaymakers from Bristol on their way to Weston-super-Mare.' The conical tower belongs to the laundry, a source of employment for many local women who could earn 1*s* a day there in 1914. *(Michael J. Tozer)*

Worle High Street, 26 June 2005. This is a very different sight from the one above, as most of the old cottages have now gone and in their place are modern shops. Of those cottages that remain, all but one have been converted into shops as well. *(Sharon Poole)*

Gunnings Stores, May 1973. This was the oldest shop in the immediate area, the chimney bearing the date 1726. From its earliest days it sold a variety of goods, from fabrics to meat. Much of the produce would have been local. There was a slaughterhouse at the rear and candles were made on the premises from the rendered pig fat or tallow. Dried goods and calicos would have been bought in. In 1826, Henry Rich established a Sunday school in the warehouse shown here on the right. To the right of the main entrance porch are steps to help people mount their horses. *(Michael J. Tozer)*

Spinners Cottages, 2005. Gunnings Stores closed in 1985 and the complex was converted for residential use. The name Spinner came from a previous owner of the shop, J.W. Spinner, who took over the business from James Irish in 1895. *(Sharon Poole)*

The Old Forge, Worle, *c.* 1968 and June 2005. This was one of two forges in Worle, the other being in Station Road. This part of Worle, together with the area at the top of the Scaurs and Church Road, is the oldest part of the village and is built on the dry, higher ground. The road sweeping round to the right is very old. It links Woodspring Priory, north of Kewstoke, to the medieval motte and bailey at Locking Head Farm. This road is very straight and both on Middle Hope and at Locking evidence of Roman occupation has been found which suggests it may be the line of a Roman road. The road down to the left is Hollow Lane, once an ancient trackway that linked the medieval fortified manor house at Castle Batch to the main village of Worle. The old forge was demolished in 1973 for road improvements. *(Above: the late E.C. Amesbury; below: Sharon Poole)*

Uphill post office, *c.* 1929. Built at the end of New Church Road, it was run by Mr Coward, pictured outside the shop. Before this building was constructed, the post office was next door in the end house of New Church Road. *(Michael J. Tozer)*

Uphill post office and stores, August 2005. Very little has changed here at all. The original post office was the white house to the left of the shop. *(Sharon Poole)*

The Ship Inn outing, 1947. This was an annual excursion for regulars of the Ship Inn at Uphill. Front row, left to right: Mrs Shepherd, Gillian Raymond, Mrs Raymond, Mrs Ellard, Elsie Huxtable, Win Ellard, Ethel Long, Mrs Middle, Annie King, Mrs Porter, Bert Middle (driver). Second row: Fred Bream, Doris Bream, -?-, Tom Tucker, -?-, Bertha Tucker, Jean Huxtable, Mrs Stevenson, Minnie Pople, Doreen Counsell, Beryl Middle, Mrs Scott, -?-, Lil Price, Bert Long. Third row: Sam Counsell (driver), H. Williams, Mr Staples, H. Raymond, -?-, -?-, Arthur Huxtable, F. Scott, H. Shepherd, David Minifie, -?-, Mrs Williams, -?-, Mrs Counsell, -?-, -?-. Back row: Derek Clark (on bus), Mrs Clark, Mr Wilshaw, Jacky Porter, -?-, -?-, -?-, Jack Hancock, H. Bowden. *(Liz Batchelor)*

Uphill Way, *c.* 1910. The original Dolphin pub burnt down in 1860 but it was soon rebuilt as in this photograph. The Ship Inn, further along the road, has been serving the people of Uphill for over 250 years. Both pubs were used by smugglers, who would guide French ships into the harbour by lantern light, and swiftly unload and hide or distribute the cargo of brandy and silks. Uphill was a busy port in its day. Cattle, slate and coal were brought in or shipped out regularly. Between the two pubs is Ynisher Terrace, built in 1911. On the left is the Old Hall, with Mr Howe and his son Charles by the gate. *(The late Ena Howe)*

Uphill Way, 2005. In spring 2004, a lot of work was carried out to improve this area, including tree felling, new seats and paths. It is one of the key areas for improvement by the Uphill Village Society. *(Sharon Poole)*

ACKNOWLEDGEMENTS

As usual a book is not just the work of one person and I am indebted to the following people for their help, information, photographs or encouragement:

The late E.C. Amesbury, Brian Austin, Liz Batchelor, Mrs Burrows, Ann Coia, Marina Coles, Laurie and Eileen Crews, Ann Deakins, Mrs G. Ellis, Mrs Elver, Jane Evans, Michael Freedman, Revd Peter Gregory, Keith Hollands, Ena Howe, Sally Huxham, Phyllis Jones, Community of La Retraite, Mary Macfarlane, Marks & Spencer Archives, North Somerset Library & Information Service, North Somerset Museum Service, Eileen Oxley, Andrew Palmer, Mr Denis Salisbury, Michael Tozer, Carol White.

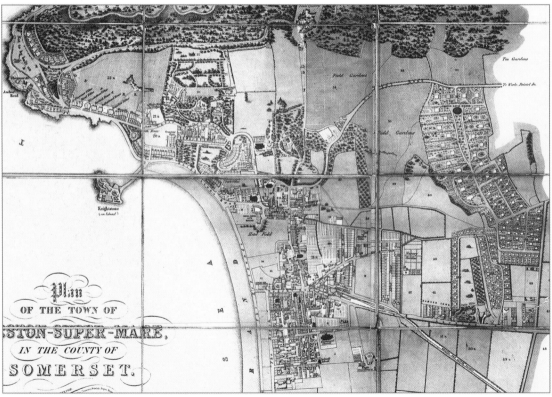

Map of Weston, early 1850s. This shows the extent of the town at this time. The southern boundary was the College, now the Grand Atlantic Hotel. To the east, new estates are shown as plots in Montpelier and Swiss Road, although the final road layouts were different from these. During the next fifty years, most of the open fields on this map were built upon. (*Sharon Poole*)